THE BEST OF NANCY POLETTE
STRATEGIES FOR READING, WRITING AND RESEARCH

Table of Contents

The Best of Nancy Polette

Strategies for
Reading, Writing and Thinking
By Nancy Polette

Pieces of
Learning

© 2003 Nancy Polette
2003 First Published by Pieces of Learning
CLC0281
ISBN 1-931334-5-3

www.piecesoflearning.com
Printed in the U.S.A.

A Note from the Publishers at Pieces of Learning

We revere Nancy Polette.

She is the Most Outstanding Role Model we know for all new teachers, librarians, reading teachers, parents, college instructors, authors, consultants, keynote speakers, mothers, wives, women, and friends. She has been all those roles to the world of women and educators.

Her character – her integrity, her sense of humor, her persistence, her energy, her creativity, her commitment, her loyalty, her trust – motivate all of us to dream our dreams and reach our goals. "That book's almost done, so what will I do next?" personifies Nancy.

Thank you, Nancy, for all you have done for the hundreds of thousands of children you have reached through their teachers. Thank you for sharing yourself with us.

Kathy Balsamo and Nancy Johnson Farris

Acknowledgements

Activities were selected from the following publications. A starred title indicates that it is, while quantities last, available from Pieces of Learning 1-800-729-5137
www.piecesoflearning.com

Activities for Any Novel*   Activities for Any Picture Book*
Bartering with Books*   Books To Begin On*
The Cay: Literature Guide*   Eight Cinderellas*
Frog and Toad Thinking Book*   Harry Potter Literature Guides*
Holes Literature Guide*   Iron Giant Literature Guide*
Multi Cultural Readers Theatre*   Predicting the Future with the Wonderful Wizard of Oz*
Pfunny Phonics*   Readers Theatre Booktalks*
Research Without Copying*   U.S. Historical Fiction*
Unforgettable Characters*   Exploring Themes in Aesop's Fables and Picture Books*
How-To Book of Literature-Based Reading*
Reading and Writing Non Fiction in the Primary Grades*
Research Book for Gifted Programs*
Research Reports to Knock Your Teachers Socks Off*

Activities with Fantasy   Best Ever Writing Models
E Is for Everybody   Enjoying Fairy Tales
Mother Goose's Animals   Multi-Cultural Literature
Reading Guidance in a Media Age   Readers Theatre
Reading the World with Folktales   Research Book of the 50 States
Research Project Book   Thinking Skills with Fairy Tales
U. History Readers Theatre   Whole Language in Action
Workshop Booklets 1990-1996

About the Illustrator . . . Paul Dillon

   When we first asked Nancy to put together her "Best" from her 100s of books and 1000s of presentations, there was no question about who could possibly provide the illustrations for her books - Paul Dillon.

   From <u>Research Without Copying</u> to his most recent collaboration with Nancy – <u>Flying with Mother Goose</u>, their first attempt together at full color – Paul has always captured on paper what dances in Nancy's mind.

   So throughout the book we've placed Paul's illustrations. Those of you familiar with Nancy's books that promote critical and creative thinking will recognize his art. Those of you new to Nancy's work can enjoy his humor.

STRATEGIES TO BUILD BRAIN POWER

What Research Says

Brain growth is due to a growing mass of connections which link neurons into efficient relay systems. New neural networks form through active interest and mental effort of the child. Every response to sights, sounds feelings, smells and tastes makes new connections.

from <u>Your Child's Growing Mind</u> by Dr. Jane Healy.
Doubleday 1987.

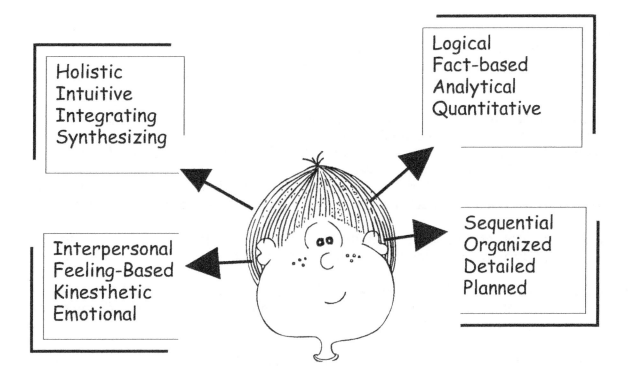

Holistic
Intuitive
Integrating
Synthesizing

Logical
Fact-based
Analytical
Quantitative

Interpersonal
Feeling-Based
Kinesthetic
Emotional

Sequential
Organized
Detailed
Planned

BRAIN COMPATIBLE TEACHING AND LEARNING

1. Take the quiz: ARE YOU A THINKER, A MOVER, A CREATOR OR A NURTURER OR ALL FOUR? Find out by taking this quiz. Answer yes or no,

___1. I follow directions well.

___2. I like things done right.   9.___Science is my favorite subject.

___3. I want to play an instrument.   10.___My desk is usually messy.

___4. I make friends easily.   11.___I like to make lists.

___5. I like non fiction books.   12.___I score well on tests.

___6. I am usually on time.   13.___I am often late.

___7. I cry at sad movies.   14.___I like to take risks.

___8. My desk is usually neat.   15.___I like working with people.

YOUR THINKING STRENGTHS

Scoring: If most of your choices were :

2,5,9,12	You are a Thinker (upper left quadrant)
1,6,8,11	You are a Mover (lower left quadrant)
3,4,7,15	You are a Nurturer (lower right quadrant)
10,13,14,16	You are a Creator (upper right quadrant)

1. The **Thinker** is strongest in the upper left quadrant of the brain. Thinkers like getting information and are very good at dealing with content.

2. The **Mover** has strength in the lower left quadrant. The Mover is organized, time conscious, a goal setter and problem solver.

3. The **Nurturer** works well with people, and likes anything that stimulates the senses, food, music, good stories, poetry and art. The Nurturer will undertake a task only if they feel like it at a given time.

4. The **Creator** is not satisfied with the status quo. The Creator is a risk taker who develops new ideas or products, likes clutter and has little use for time.

According to the research of Dr. Ned Hermann (The Creative Brain, Applied Creative Services Ltd. 1986), 95% of adults show greater strength in two quadrants over the other two; 5% show equal ability in all four.

Activity Identify the major thinking strengths of Dorothy, the Lion, the Tinman and the Scarecrow from The Wizard of Oz. Why was their journey so successful?

TEACHING TO ALL FOUR QUADRANTS OF THE BRAIN

1. Use of meaningful content. (Upper left quadrant)

2. Goal based instruction that allows the learner to organize content in new ways. (Lower left quadrant)

3. Encouragement of risk-taking (guessing) and development of original ideas and products. (Upper right quadrant)

4. Learning from others in groups. Use of music, literature, art. (Lower right quadrant)

The strategies that follow are designed to stimulate thinking in all four brain quadrants and can be used with **any print** at **any level.**

READING, WRITING & REASONING STRATEGIES

1. **Topic Talking** Assign partners. Partner A speaks to partner B on a topic given by the teacher (and related to the selection to be read) for 10 seconds. The teacher then says "switch" and B speaks to A on the topic for 10 seconds. The teacher says stop and then gives a second topic. The same procedure is followed but speaking time can be increased. Over a period of weeks, gradually increase the size of the group so that one child is speaking to two others, then three others etc. <u>Purpose</u>: To get students to share experiences about what they will be reading and to develop oral language facility.

2. **Categorizing New Vocabulary** Provide small groups of students with a list of vocabulary words and categories in which to place the words. Guessing is encouraged.

   Example Decide if each of these words from <u>The Wizard of Oz</u> is
   (1) an object (2) a person (3) a plant (4) an animal

   ___ greensward   ___ snood   ___ Boq   ___ kalidah
   ___ counterpane   ___ mendicant   ___ caroche   ___ kerria
   ___ peplos

Read to support or deny guesses.

   Dorothy untangled herself from the counterpane on the bed and threw it aside. She walked outside the house stepping around the sweet-smelling rose kerria bush and stared in awe at the rich greensward that surrounded her. Boq, the leader of the Munchkins, bid her welcome. Then in a burst of light Glenda, the good witch, stepped from a gold caroche pulled by six white horses. A glittering snood covered her hair and the peplos around her shoulders was made of silver thread. Dorothy now became the mendicant, asking Glenda's help to return home. Glenda gave Dorothy silver shoes to protect her from the kalidah beasts, the wicked witch of the West and other dangers.

3. Giant Sentences Show one illustration from the story. Working in small groups, students use a list of vocabulary words to use in ONE sentence to describe the visual.

Words to describe a visual from The Wizard of Oz are:

prairie	whirlwind	cyclone	amazement	kalidah
luscious	Munchkins	sorceress	hesitate	bondage
civilized	journey	curious	danger	earnest
tedious	discouraged	weapon	patient	oblige
enchanted	anxious	awkward	enable	clumsy
destroy	industrious	monstrous	reproach	mishap
wolves	witch	dangerous	misfortune	cruelty
inconvenient	astonished	motionless	aroused	weapons
reflection	spectacles	companions	assistance	dismal
prosperous	fragrance	telescope	confidential	

4. Pre Reading Journals Provide students with open-ended sentence starters for the story or novel chapters to be read. These are related in general to what the students will be reading. Students choose one to write about for five minutes. Then students get into small pre-assigned groups and read aloud what they have written.

Sample Pre Reading Sentence Starters for The Wizard of Oz:

Chapter One: The Cyclone
    1. Living on the prairie in a one room house . . .
    2. Cyclones are scary because . . .
Chapter Two: The Council with the Munchkins
    3. Waking up in a strange place can be . . .
    4. In a civilized country people usually . . .
Chapter Three: How Dorothy Saved the Scarecrow
    5. When strangers offer hospitality . . .
    6. A lighted match can cause trouble when . . .

5. Find Someone Who The student relates past experiences to the literature. List 7-10 statements related in general to the story or novel to be read. Students must find someone in the class to fit each statement.

Example Find Someone Who
A) Is wearing something green _____
B) Has visited Kansas _____
C) Has been more than 1000 miles from home. _____
D) Has a name that begins with D. _____
E) Has met a difficult challenge. _____
F) Can do a magic trick. _____
G) Likes yellow better than any other color. _____

6. Anticipation/Reaction Guide The teacher lists six to eight statements or commonly held beliefs related to the selection to be read. Working in small groups students put plus and minus signs indicating their agreement or disagreement with each statement. After reading the selection they again rate the statements plus or minus.

Primary
_____ A pig would make a good pet. _____
_____ Spiders are not useful insects. _____
_____ Rats cause trouble on farms. _____
     (Charlotte's Web)

Intermediate
_____ Adults are not to be trusted. _____
_____ The only one you can depend on is yourself. _____
_____ A mother would never abandon her child. _____
     (The Great Gilly Hopkins)

7. Missing Paragraphs From a short story or an incident in a novel, duplicate a passage and cut apart in paragraphs. Distribute all but the first paragraph to partners. The teacher reads the first paragraph. The partners who think they have the next paragraph read until the entire passage is read.

8. Finish the Story The teacher reads the story up to the last paragraph. Duplicate and distribute the last paragraph with missing words. Students work together to add the words they think best fit. Then read aloud the last paragraph from the story.

9. Skills from the Text Select a skill for a mini lesson.
  Example Kinds of sentences, kinds of nouns - common, proper, singular, collective, possessive etc. Ask students to find examples in their reading selections.
  Example Who can find an interrogative sentence? Who can find a sentence that contains a common, proper and a possessive noun in the same sentence? Who can find a sentence that is a fact? An opinion?

10. Inferring After reading give small groups or partners clue cards. Cards are labeled location, occupations, time, feelings. Students find and read aloud specific sentences that provide clues to the word on their cards.
  Example Find a sentence that tells you the time of year the story takes place.

11. <u>Cause and Effect</u> List incidents from the story.

    <u>Example</u> from <u>Dakota Dugout</u> (by Ann Turner) one might list: <u>talked to sparrows</u>, <u>pasted newspaper on the walls</u>, <u>built a sod house</u>. Students are to work together to list at least one cause and one effect for each incident.

12. <u>Topic Focusing</u> Working in small groups, students are given a topic related to a non fiction reading selection. Groups guess the answers to the questions, then read to support or deny guesses.

    <u>Example</u> To introduce <u>The BFG</u> (by Roald Dahl) series which takes place in England:
    A. Great Britain is how many miles long?_____
    B. Great Britain is how many miles wide?_____
    C. How many ruling kings has Great Britain had since 1707?_____
    D. How many ruling queens ?_____
    E. Great Britain has ___times as many people as live in Oregon.

<u>Read to support or deny guesses.</u>

    Great Britain is the largest island in Europe and the seventh largest island in the world. While it is nearly the same size as Oregon, it has thirty times as many people. The distance from east to west is 320 miles. The distance from north to south is 600 miles. From 1707 when Scotland, England and Wales were joined, Great Britain has had nine ruling kings and three ruling queens.

13. <u>Word Game</u> To create new people. places and objects the author must also create new words.

    <u>Example</u> In the Harry Potter books what do you think these new words might describe?

        Locomotor Mortis   Finite Incantum   Patronus Charm   Serpensortial

    Combine two of the words that follow to make a compound word. Tell how this word would fit at Hogwarts.

bridge	foot	box	mail	cast	porch	sun	book	man
rain	potion	fish	cat	pick	card	note	stick	arrow
water	feather							

    <u>Example</u> <u>Footpick</u>: a small tool to attach to the big toe used in digging gardens.

14. <u>Rank Order</u> In groups of four, students list their favorite items related to the story. These might be <u>food</u>, <u>clothing</u>, <u>sports</u>, <u>books</u> or <u>activities</u>. Each member lists two items. The group must then rank order the items from the ones the **group** likes most to least.

    <u>Example</u> <u>The Iron Giant</u> (by Ted Hughes) was destroying the farmer's crops. Each student lists two favorite foods that come from a farm. The group rank orders the list from most to least favorite.

15. <u>Shared Reading</u> The shared reading experience consists of a model reader reading aloud while others join in. In primary grades "big books," those with print large enough to be seen at a distance, are often used. Overhead transparencies also work well. The model reader should read slowly enough so that children can follow the line of print as the reader's hand moves along the line. Model reading includes pausing at appropriate points in the text and using the rise or fall of the voice appropriately. Shared reading materials can include the text of a story, poetry, song lyrics, chants or any other material.

<u>**Techniques**</u> for shared reading include:

Repetition Sharing the story or poem many times.
Patterning Selecting stories or poems with repeating patterns.
Echo Reading Reading a line from a poem and having children repeat or echo the line.
Tracking Moving the hand or finger along the line being read as children listen to establish the connection between what they are seeing and what they are hearing.
Fading As children grow confident in their ability to read the text the model reader gradually softens his/her voice and stops reading while the young readers continue.

16. <u>Partnership Reading</u>
   A. Demonstrate the predictive reading lesson with the class showing students how to use questions that predict action. Then assign reading partners. (partners do not have to have the same reading level)
   B. Assign individual reading selections based on student interest and ability. (Can be self-selected if appropriate to the reading level of the student) Assign independent reading time. Call stop after 3-5 minutes. Have each student write one question that has arisen and a possible answer, or tell the reading partner what has happened in the story and what question needs to be answered now.
   C. Continue independent reading. At the conclusion of the reading, students share with partners:
      1. Story summary.
      2. What they thought would happen.
      3. What did happen.
   D. Oral reading. Each student reads aloud a favorite page to his/her partner.
   E. Students volunteer to read aloud to the class a favorite paragraph.

17. <u>Predictive Reading</u> Read the following story (The Contented Old Woman p. 8) aloud or make a transparency and read together with students. Uncover only that portion of the transparency you are reading. Stop at appropriate points and ask for predictions. Check to see if the student has a reason for the prediction.

<u>**Predictive questions to ask**</u> Ask about what will be read, not what has been read.
   A. What does the title mean?
   B. What will the story be about?
   C. What is the problem?
   D. What will happen next?
   E. Why do you predict that?
   F. What are other possibilities?
   G. Given what you know, what do you think will be the outcome?
   H. How can we find out?

The Contented Old Woman

One day a poor old woman was digging potatoes in her garden. All at once she stooped and pulled out of the earth a big iron pot full of gold. She was pleased as she could be.

She dragged it a little way toward her house and looked again to make sure that it was full of gold. What do you think she found?

The gold had turned into silver! She was as pleased as she could be. She dragged it a little further and had to stop for breath. She looked again to make sure it was full of silver. What do you suppose had happened?

The silver had turned to copper pennies. Still she was as pleased as she could be. At the door she looked again to make sure that she had her pennies safe. Well, what do you think she saw?

There was nothing in the pot but a heavy stone. She remembered that she needed just such a stone to keep her door open. She was still as pleased as she could be. As she stooped to pick up the stone, what do you suppose happened?

The stone turned into a hideous dragon breathing fire. He jumped over her flower beds and flew away. Do you think the old woman was cross then?

No, she clapped her hands and cried, "Oh, how lucky I am! He might have eaten me up, house and garden and all!" So the contented old woman baked potatoes for supper and went to sleep in her cozy bed.

18. Group Discussion Questions Using these beginnings: How many ways, What if, If you were? How is _____ like _____? give small groups one question related to the story. The group assigns a recorder to list main ideas and discusses the question for 10 minutes. At the end of discussion time, ideas are shared with the class.
   Example How many ways is the story of The Wizard of Oz like the tale of Hansel and Gretel?

Four Levels Of Discussion Questions

By using the questions that follow with any literature selection, the teacher should see a deepening of the levels of response and a growing awareness on the part of students that literature is a way by which one can experience life and commonality among all mankind. Not all questions need to be asked. Use those most appropriate to the literature selection.
   After students have been guided through the questioning process by the teacher, literature discussion groups can be formed for other selections. Students can use these questions as a guide in their self-directed group discussions.

Objective

1. What words or phrases do you remember?
2. What people do you remember seeing?
3. What colors, objects, sounds, textures do you recall?

Reflective

4. Whom did you like or dislike in the story?
5. With whom did you identify?
6. What emotions did you see in the story? When?
7. What kind of music would you choose to accompany this story?

Interpretative

8. Was there any point in the story when you felt happy? sad? apprehensive? angry? disappointed?
9. If you could have stopped the story at any point, where would you have stopped it?
10. If you needed to shorten the story where would you have made the cuts?

Decisional

11. How do you think the main character felt at the end of the story?
12. Have you ever felt like this?
13. Who needs to read this story? (Think of an historical figure or another character from literature).
14. If you could be any of the characters, which would you choose to be?
15. What title would you give this story?

19. <u>Summarizing the Story</u> Use this form for analyzing any story and for developing your own story.

TITLE_____   **Author** _____

CHARACTERS   **Short Description**

1._____

2._____

3._____

4._____

SETTING _____

When _____ Length of time passed_____

PLOT State the story problem

_____

_____

List three events that took place before the problem was solved.

1._____

2._____

3._____

How was the problem solved? _____

_____

THEME

What important idea did the author try to convey in this story?

_____

What did a character do to convey this idea?

_____

What happened in the plot to support this idea?

_____

20. <u>Responding in Poetry or Song</u> Students take a familiar tune and summarize the plot of the story or novel.

Summarizing <u>Charlotte's Web</u> by E. B. White

A Song About Charlotte
Sing to the tune of "My Bonnie Lies Over the Ocean."

Verse:
Oh, this is a song about Charlotte
A spider so gentle and good,
Who promised a small pig named Wilbur
She'd save him if anyone could.

Chorus:
Wilbur, Charlotte
And Templeton lived on a tidy farm
Charlotte promised
To rescue poor Wilbur from harm.

Verse:
Now Fern sold her uncle the piglet
He then tried to fatten the beast
To take a plump pig to the butcher
And turn him into a ham feast

Verse:
So Charlotte spins a wordy message
To tell the world about her friend,
And Wilbur is saved from the butcher
To bring this fine tale to an end.

Sing to the tune of "Skip To My Lou."
Use the pattern for any story.

<u>Adjective</u>	<u>Noun</u>	<u>"ing" word</u>	<u>Prepositional phrase</u>
<u>Example</u>			
Worried	Wilbur	walking	in the barn
Helpful	Charlotte	spinning	in her web
Greedy	Templeton	watching	in the kitchen
Read, little children, read.			

21. The "I Have, Who Has?" Game

An "I Have, Who Has?" game can be constructed for any story. Cut apart the boxes and distribute randomly about the class. The student with the starred card reads the WHO HAS portion of the card. By listening carefully, students should be able to respond correctly even if they have not read the story. ** Starts the game.

I HAVE: "I was your washerwoman". ** WHO HAS: Where does the story "Tomorrow" take place?	I HAVE: The strong woman felt at home where everything was friendly. WHO HAS: What did the frightened woman ask of the strong woman?
I HAVE: "Tomorrow" takes place in the Land of the Great Beyond. WHO HAS: Where did the two women meet?	I HAVE: The frightened woman asked to hold the strong woman's hand. WHO HAS: What was the frightened woman's life like on earth?
I HAVE: The two women met by the golden gates. WHO HAS: What did the two women look like?	I HAVE: On earth the frightened woman was a rich lady with jewels and servants. WHO HAS: How did the frightened woman feel about coming to this new place?
I HAVE: One woman was strong and beautiful and the other was pinched and gray. WHO HAS: How did the pinched and gray woman feel?	I HAVE: The frightened woman did not want to come. She felt terrible. WHO HAS: How did the strong woman feel about coming to this strange new place?
I HAVE: The pinched and gray woman trembled with fright. WHO HAS: Why was the gray woman afraid?	I HAVE: The strong woman came willingly. WHO HAS: What did the frightened woman notice about the strong woman?
I HAVE: The gray woman was afraid of being alone in a strange place. WHO HAS: How did the strong woman feel?	I HAVE: The frightened woman thought she had met the strong woman before. WHO HAS: How did the strong woman identify herself? *

22. The Storyboard

1. On the storyboard below are ten spaces. Space one is the character/setting space. Write the names of the characters and the setting in space one.

2. Cut apart the incident cards. These are the incidents that move the story along. Choose one you think will fit in space two.

3. Space three is the problem. Briefly state the problem to be solved in space three.

4. Space eight should be the most exciting point in the story.

5. Space ten concludes the story.

6. Continue moving the story along by placing incident cards in the empty spaces. By the time you reach space ten you should have solved the problem in space three. When the storyboard is completed you are ready to write your story!

Fill the blank spaces on the storyboard below with the incident cards. Be sure in developing the story that the problem (space 3) and solution (space 10) match!

Storyboard

1.Character / Setting A witch and an elf on a country road.	6.
2.	7.
3. Problem: The witch wants the elf to do something but the elf refuses.	8.
4.	9.
5.	10. Solution

Incident Cards

A bargain is made	It rains	Someone walks away
Someone runs	A bus arrives	A giant appears
An invitation arrives	The order is given	An animal escapes
A bottle is found	The cloud covers the sun	A magic ring is found
The earth trembles	There is silence	The load was heavy
They travel together	The sun comes up	Someone smiles
Someone sings	It is caught	Someone screams
Footsteps are heard	A bird appears	The search begins
The fight begins	The noise gets louder	They can't find it
It is invisible	It drops	It is fixed

23. Debate Each team has a set period of time to debate an issue.
   Example From <u>Death of the Iron Horse</u> (by Paul Goble) debate: The railroads had a right to cross Indian lands. The class votes on the team with the best arguments. OR list pros and cons (an equal number of each) on an issue.

24. Evaluate Select a main character from the story or novel. List personal traits to evaluate in the character (can be done report card style), <u>courage</u>, <u>determination</u>, <u>perseverance</u>, <u>caring</u>, etc. Give a grade for each trait and a comment justifying each grade.

25. Character Traits Choose a character from a story or novel. Write four characteristics of the character. Under each characteristic give at least three pieces of evidence from the story for each of the traits.

   Example <u>Stone Fox</u> (by John Gardimer)
   <u>Character</u>: Stone Fox
   <u>Trait</u>:   Experienced   Why? Won every race. People bet on him.
   <u>Trait</u>:   Caring   Why? Stopped the race. Let Wilie win.

26. The One Hour Novel A novel is distributed to partners. Each pair of students is assigned a different chapter to read. They summarize the chapter using the form that follows. Summaries are then read in order.
   Chapter ____ takes place ____. ____ is an important character and can be described as ____. Another character is _____ and can be described as _____. In this chapter the action starts when _____. After that _____ and _____. The chapter ends with _____.

27. Data Banks
Give students the data bank headings you want them to use, Each must find three to five items of information to go under each heading. Headings for an animal report follow:

Alligator Data Bank

<u>Eats</u>	<u>Has</u>	<u>Does</u>
fish	thick body	makes nest of grass
snakes	sharp teeth	lays 50 eggs at a time
dogs	short, strong legs	grows about one foot a
frogs	powerful tail	year
turtles	tough skin	rests under water in
		winter
		lives 50-60 years

<u>Lives</u>	<u>Looks Like</u>
SE United States	lizard
China	18 feet long
Central America	450-550 pounds
South America	dull gray or dark olive color

---

28. The Research Report

The student can show understanding of non fiction text by using the information in a pattern report (see the pattern section of this book) **or** The student produces a clearly written, well organized research report on any topic by using the organizing procedure that follows.

THE DATA BANK AND RESEARCH REPORT

1. Give students the Data Bank headings you want them to research. A minimum of five details or facts must be found for each heading.

2. Suggested headings:
   FOR PEOPLE   Family, Life, Description, Beliefs, Accomplishments
   FOR PLACES   Location, Climate, Wildlife, Products, Attractions, People
   FOR EVENTS   Location, Description, Purpose, People Involved, Results, Other Facts
   FOR ANIMALS   Location, Food, Physical Characteristics, Enemies, Habits
   (For grades one and two use: Eats, Lives, Has, Does)

3. Data Bank information is transferred to cards or a chart.

Data Bank Heading

Card

Note_____

Why?_____

Like or unlike what?_____

Source_____

Write the report by putting all items for one heading in the same paragraph. Decide which item is most important. That item will be the topic sentence.

Chart

Notes	Why?	Like or Unlike

29. Productive Thinking For example, using the <u>Frog and Toad</u> picture books (by Arnold Lobel)

A. <u>FLUENCY</u> Brainstorm many responses
1. How many words can you think of to describe a toad?
2. How many uses can you name for twenty-five bags of leaves?

B. <u>FLEXIBILITY</u> Stretch the mind beyond the expected response; finding new uses for materials; finding new categories for grouping
1. How many ways can you group the words listed in Column A?
2. How can Frog use any of these items to get Toad out of bed? pail of water, feather, bag of popcorn, a drum, a book. Remember, Frog wants Toad to be his friend.

C. <u>ORIGINALITY</u> Respond in new or unique ways.
Choose one item from each box. Think of an original way to end the story that no one else with think of.

<u>Once there was</u>	<u>Who was</u>
A talking toad A young prince A butterfly A poor girl	Eating lunch Running a race Look for a friend Crying
<u>When</u>	<u>So</u>
It began to rain A knight rode by A magic door opened Trees began to talk	Give the story an original ending.

D. <u>ELABORATION</u> Add to a product to enhance it or make it more complete.
The animals said Toad looked funny in his bathing suit. What could you add to it so that every animal would want one just like I?

See examples of elaboration in books by Larry Shles: <u>Hoots and Toots and Hairy Brutes</u> and <u>Nose Drops</u> (Jalmar, 1998).

30. Critical Thinking (with historical fiction)

I. PLANNING - Identify steps, materials, and problems necessary

A. You are an apprentice to a silversmith in the late 1700s. You have an opportunity to show your latest work to a well-known client who will pay a lot for it if it is completed by Monday. This means that to complete it you will have to work on Sunday . . . Sunday work is forbidden in the colonies. Plan how you will complete the task. Include steps, time table, materials needed and possible problems.

B. In the book Johnny Tremain, Johnny is faced with this task. In rushing to complete the task he spills molten silver on his hand and becomes permanently crippled. He can no longer make beautiful silver items. Plan a future for Johnny that will allow him to use his artistic talent with only one hand. Read Johnny Tremain (by Esther Forbes).

II. FORECASTING - Link cause and effect

What might cause one person to take credit for the work or achievements of another? What would be the effects of having another person take credit for your work?

In Ben and Me and Mr. Revere and I, author Robert Lawson presents humorous accounts of Ben, the mouse, who claims he gave Ben Franklin all the great invention ideas and of Sherry, the horse, who laments the fact that without him, Paul Revere could never have made the famous ride.

III. EVALUATION - Examine positive and negative aspects

A. Suppose you could trade places with a character in your favorite historical fiction book. What would be the advantages? What would be the disadvantages?

B. Evaluate an historical movie or television show you have seen. What was good about it? What was poor?

IV. DECISION MAKING - Establish and apply criteria for making choices

You have time-tripped back to 1789. You know there are many things that are a part of your life today that could make life better for those in 1789. What **one** thing will you share to improve the quality of life in this new nation?

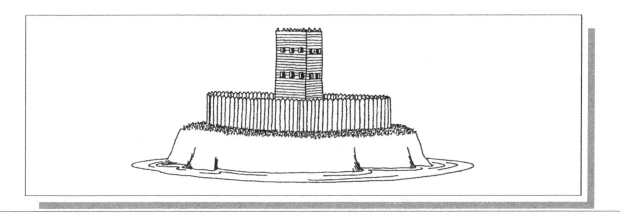

31. <u>Problem Solving</u> Every story has a problem that must be solved. Read a story to the point where the problem arises. **Before** finishing the story to see how the author solves the problem, try solving the problem by using the steps listed below. Then finish the story. Did you like your solution better? The author's? Were they the same?

1. What important facts can you state about the situation?

_____

_____

2. State the major problem.

_____

3. List as many ways as you can to deal with the problem. These are your <u>alternatives</u>.

_____

_____

_____

_____

4. Select the four best ideas and enter them on the decision grid below.
5. Two criteria for judging ideas are provided in the grid. Add a third of your own.
6. Evaluate each idea on a scale of one to five. A poor rating is one; a high rating is five.

Title _____ Author _____

Story Problem: _____

Best Ideas	Is It Fast?	Is It Possible?		Scale 1-5 Total

18

32. <u>Pick A Project!</u> A Research Organizer

Step One	**Step Two**	**Step Three**
Choose and circle one action word	Choose and circle one topic	Choose and circle one product
Label	(Brainstorm with the class topics to list here that are related to the litera- ture selection you are reading or are related to a non-fiction research project. List as many topics as you can.)	Acrostic poem
List		Chart
Describe		Story
Locate		Model
Report		Map
Show	**Example**	Mobile
Group	If a topic listed here was "Heart Transplants" (what the Tinman wanted in <u>The Wizard of Oz</u>), I might decide to report on the first doctor to perform a heart transplant as a Bio-Poem or an Interview.	Diorama
Discover		Bio-poem
Compose		Report
Create		True/false book
Demonstrate		Drawing
Choose		
Tell About		

Write a sentence telling what you will do to report on the topic you choose. In your sentence include an action word and a product as well as your topic.

action	topic	product

_____

_____

_____

PUTTING IT ALL TOGETHER: MISS MUFFET REVISITED

Each of the activities that follow is labeled with the number of the strategy that is used and the quadrant of the brain that is stimulated to action.

Find Someone Who . . .
Find one person in the group for each line below. Write the person's first name on the line. A name can be used only once. **(Strategy #5 Lower right)**

Find someone who . . .

1. Knows what whey is. _____

2. Has had a spider as a pet. _____

3. Does not like spiders. _____

4. Has eaten lunch outdoors. _____

5. Has a tuffet at home. _____

6. Has visited France. _____

7. Can name something written by Charles Perrault. _____

8. Has held a spider in his or her hand. _____

See if you can come up with the magic number! Talk the answers over with a friend. **Guess** if you do not know the answer. Then listen to the poem to support or deny your guesses. **(Strategy # 12 upper right)**

1. How many legs does a spider have? _____

2. How many eyes does a spider have? _____

3. How many parts does the body of a spider have? _____

4. How many rows of eyes does a spider have? _____

                                                    Total _____

Support or deny guesses by reading the poem on the next page.

The answers to the spider questions are found in this poem. It is fun to read aloud to scary music. **(Strategy #20 lower right.)**

Little Miss Muffet
Sat on a tuffet
Eating her curds and whey.
Along came a spider
And sat down beside her
And frightened Miss Muffet away.

The young Miss looked down
On her face was a frown.
Determined to have her own way,
She looked at the creature
And marked every feature,
While holding it gently at bay.

She measured its size
And counted eight eyes,
Two body parts and eight long legs.
With eyes in two rows
And missing a nose,
"Stop eating my supper" she begs.

"Do you think I'm a fool?"
Asked the spider so cool,
"I will eat just as much as I can.
"No, you won't" she insists,
And she raised up her fists,
"For you see I've come up with a plan!"

LET'S DO A SPIDER PROJECT! (Strategy #32 Upper left)

Choose A Verb	Choose a Topic	Choose a Product
List	Crab spider	Poem
Describe	Ground spider	Song
Show	Jumping spider	Drawing
Create	Stick spider	Fact or Fiction Book
Judge	Tarantula	Pattern Report
Compare	Wolf spider	

PROBLEM SOLVING: HELP MISS MUFFET GET RID OF THE SPIDER

(Strategy 31: Lower left)
List your best ideas on the lines below. Evaluate each idea using the criteria. If the answer is YES, put a 3 in the box. If the answer is NO, put a 1 in the box. If the answer is MAYBE, put a 2 in the box. The first idea is scored for you.

Criteria

Your Ideas	Fast?	Low Cost?	Safe	Effective	Total
Get a can of Raid	2	1	3	3	9

Total the scores by adding across. The idea with the largest score is the one to try first!
Our best idea is _____

Write a final verse to tell what your solution is.

Here is one example

With time to give thought

And to do what she ought,

Miss Muffet returned that same day.

Though she would grow thinner,

She picked up her dinner,

And buried the spider in whey.

A PATTERN FOR REPORTING ON SPIDERS

A beginning research project. **(Strategy #28 Upper left, lower left)**
Students examine books about spiders, noting the name of one spider and where it is found.
The information is used in the pattern that follows.
(The same pattern can be used for any topic that requires a list.)

WRITE A SPIDER CHANT

I like spiders!

(list the names of six kinds of spiders)

1. crab spiders

2. _____

3. _____

4. _____

5. _____

6. _____

These are just a few...

(now list seven places spiders are found)

1. in the grass

2. _____

3. _____

4. _____

5. _____

6. _____

7. _____, too!

Stand and shout!

Don't let them out!

I like spiders!

Example

I like spiders!
    Crab spiders
    Ground spiders
    Jumping spiders
    Stick spiders
    Wolf spiders
    Tarantulas
These are just a few!

    In a web
    Underground
    On a flower
    In the house
    Between the leaves
    In the grass
    Trapdoor spiders, too!

Stand and shout!
Don't let them out!
I like spiders!

A THINKING SKILLS QUIZ

PRODUCTIVE THINKING #29	PROBLEM SOLVING #31	CRITICAL THINKING # 30	
The student expresses many ideas though not all of the highest quality. (Fluency)	The student gives many alternatives to a problem solution	The student can determine the causes and effects of a given situation (Forecasting)	The student is able to look at the parts of a whole and the relationships among parts. (Analyze)
The student can group items in a variety of ways.(Flexibility)	The student is able to weigh alternatives using selected criteria.	The student is able to define the basic attributes of a person, place or thing. (Attribute Listing)	The student is able to find common elements among seemingly dissimilar items. (Analogy)
The student expresses unusual or uncommon responses, though not all ideas prove to be of use. (Originality)	The student is able to make a final judgment in terms of alternatives.		
The student builds onto a basic idea or product by adding details to make it more interesting or complete. (Elaboration)	The student is able to defend his/her decision by giving many reasons for the choice.		The student is able to examine data, draw a generalization and support or deny generalizations with evidence. (Generalize)

Put the number of each assignment below in the Strategy Box above which best shows the type of thinking required.

1. Give six unusual ways for Frog to get Toad out of bed and keep his friendship.
2. Prepare a chart on European folktales showing character, setting, plot & theme of each. Examine the completed chart. What broad statements can you make about European folktales?
3. List all the words you can to describe Ebenezer Scrooge.
4. After reading <u>Mr. Popper's Penguins</u>, create a data bank about penguins.
5. Discuss the many ways that Hatchet by Paulsen and Grimm's Snow White are alike.
6. Use evidence from the story to predict what will happen next.
7. How many ways can you group books by Walter Dean Myers?
8. How can Miss Muffet get rid of the spider? Give several ideas.
9. Give reasons for and against selling candy to raise money for your school.
10. Add sounds or words to the first verse of Paul Revere's Ride to make it livelier.
11. Apply numerical values to listed ideas as to how Willy (in <u>Stone Fox</u>) can earn 500 dollars to pay the taxes on the farm.
12. Create character comparisons using this pattern: <u>Mary Poppins</u> is to <u>nice</u> as the <u>Wicked Witch of the West</u> is to <u>mean</u>.
13. What would be the best way for Pinocchio to escape from the belly of the whale?

Key: Productive: 3,7,1,10   Problem Solving: 8,11,13,9,6,4   Critical Thinking 5,12,2

EVALUATION

Assessing student responses

The reader-response activities on the pages that follow are related to specific chapters in a novel. The activities can be done individually or by groups, and encompass a wide variety of reading, writing and thinking skills within many subject disciplines.

If desired, a ten-point score can be given for successful completion of each activity. Use the scoring criteria given below. Be sure the student or group has a list of the criteria before doing the activity. Grades can be assigned according to the number of points the student or group accumulates during the novel study.

If grades are not necessary or desirable, these activities are excellent additions to the student's reading/language art portfolio. Samples of student work should show not only progress throughout the year, but progress from the beginning to the end of a novel. The activities encompass writing samples, both narrative and expository, creative response projects, divergent products and related reading. In addition, the portfolio should contain lists of books read and a written record of the individual reading conference.

How To Score

Give the student the criteria appropriate for his/her project. When the project is complete the student scores himself/herself. The scoring is handed in with the project. Then the teacher scores the project. If there is a wide difference in scores on individual items the teacher and student have a conference to resolve the difference. Score **1** = **no** to **10** = **yes**

Evaluation of Original Stories

___ Shows a concept of plot (story has a beginning, middle, end)
___ Relates setting to plot
___ Describes characters in several ways
___ Shows logical sequence of action
___ Story problem easily identified
___ Use of descriptive language
___ Major and minor ideas are consistent
___ Clear transition between ideas
___ Correct spelling/grammar
___ Creative problem solution
___ Neatness/completed on time

Evaluation of Written Research Products

___ Use of a variety of sources
___ All facts verified by listed sources
___ Clarity of expression
___ Logical progression of ideas
___ Inclusion of important details
___ Bibliography of sources of information
___ Information presented in a creative manner
___ Neatness
___ Paper's conclusions make sense

Evaluation of Non Written Products

___ Uses of a variety of sources
___ Presents core materials in a creative way
___ Attention to detail
___ Good design (compostition)
___ How the eye is drawn
___ Logical connection between topic and product
___ Labels and lettering neat and correctly spelled
___ Information easy to understand
___ Accompanied by a list of sources of information
___ Correct use of language
___ Neatness

Comments

SHARING PICTURE BOOKS

Writers with profound messages and artistic brilliance are focusing their creative talents in picture books for children. Although we cannot, however dedicated we are and no matter how hard we try, be in tune with all of the active mental meanderings and discoveries which our students are experiencing, we can lure children to meet gifted writers and illustrators. We can introduce them to those who over many decades have spoken through the pages of literature to the greatness within those who are listening. Lively, creative minds are writing today as well, and we need but to get their works into children's hands.

What young reader has not discovered the value of friendship with Arnold Lobel's <u>Frog and Toad</u> series? How many of us can identify with Squib from Larry Shles's <u>Hoots and Toots and Hairy Brutes</u>? At first the little owl pines away because he cannot hoot, but in the end his little "toot" is as valuable as any big "hoot" in the forest. The devastation of war combined with one's responsibility toward others brings a powerful message in Jane Cutler's <u>Cello of Mr. O</u>. Smiles abound with the sharing of <u>The Mightiest</u> or <u>The Wolf's Chicken Stew</u> by Keiko Kasza as the serious issues of bullying and misuse of power are handled in a gentle yet effective way.

There are those who would ask,"Do children really need a literature program? Surely,

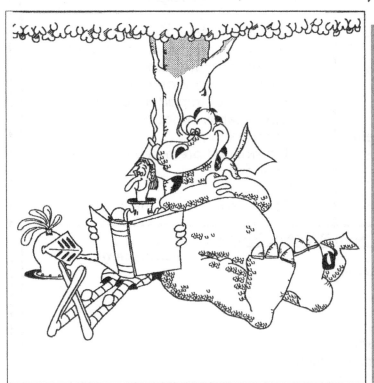

children who started reading early and are already fluent in written language can find their own way." Marjorie Hamelin writes in <u>Reading Guidance in a Media Age</u> "Those of us who have gone down a rabbit hole, climbed the mast of a plunging schooner with a pirate hot on our tails, learned to breathe under water on a Martian moon — those of us who have done these things realize how narrow and bleak our lives would have been if untouched by these mind-stretching adventures. Beyond the skills of learning to read lies a land of vision and enchantment. A child who is never pointed in that direction may grow to adulthood literate in only the "letters" sense of the word, and with a sadly undernourished spirit. "

Picture books are the first course of the literary feast that every child deserves. But picture books are not just for primary students!

VISUAL LITERACY

It is a **myth** that constant exposure to a fact or concept means that one will learn.
- A. Does the head on a penny face right or left?
- B. Does the Statue of Liberty hole her torch in her right or left hand?
- C. When you fold your arms, which hand is tucked in?
- D. When you clasp your hands, which thumb is on top?

When looking at illustrations ask **key questions** to interpret an artist's purpose.
- A. **LINE**: What lines indicate stillness? (vertical/horizontal). What lines show movement? (diagonal). What lines are repeated?
- B. **COLOR**: Where are the darkest colors? Lightest colors? What feelings do we associate with dark and light colors? Is color used to foreshadow coming action?
- C. **SHAPE/SIZE**: What is the largest item in the print? The smallest? How does size show distance? Is size used to indicate what is most important in the print?
- D. **FRAMES**: Are any objects framed in the print? Why?

Use these **outstanding books** to promote visual literacy.
Agee, John. The Incredible Painting of Felix Clousseau. Farrar, 1988.
Anno. Anno's Journey, Anno's Britain, Anno's U.S.A. Philomel, 1986-1988.
Dunbar, Fiona. You'll Never Guess. Dial 1991.
Marshall, James. Red Riding Hood. Dial, 1991.
Polette, Nancy. The Hole by the Apple Tree. Greenwillow, 1992.
Rockwell, Anne. Albert B Cub and Zebra. Crowell, 1977.

Interpreting visuals beyond the literal level. For Middle School/Junior High share Sylvester and the Magic Pebble by William Steig. Simon & Schuster, 1969.

Summary

Sylvester, a donkey, finds a pebble that makes wishes come true. One day in the meadow he meets a lion, and without thinking, he wishes he were a stone. The puzzled lion looks at the stone and walks away. However, the pebble rolls away from the stone and Sylvester cannot wish himself to be a donkey again. He remains in this state for an entire year until spring when his father takes his mother on a picnic to cheer her up. She finds the pebble, lays it on the stone, and a happy family reunion ensues.

Divide the class into groups of three to five students. After sharing the book with the class, ask each group to select from the headlines below, the one which is most closely related to the story. The group should discuss and list as many ways as possible how the headline it selects and the story are related.

Social Welfare Fund Tops Goal   Local Drug Raid A Success
Prison Overcrowding A Problem   Oil Companies Increase Profits
Local Factory Closes: Many Seek Jobs Elsewhere
Legislators Debate Gun Control Law

BOOKS TO BEGIN ON

1. IS THIS A HOUSE FOR HERMIT CRAB? by Megan McDonald. Illustrated by S.D. Schindler. Orchard, 1990.

Hermit Crab is looking for a new home. Scritch, scratch he goes along the shore, by the sea, in the sand. But each home he finds has something wrong with it.

Poetry Pattern (Choose a creature found in the ocean to complete the pattern.)
I saw a _____ and the _____ saw me.
It was _____ along in the deep, blue sea.
_____ goes _____ _____ _____

2. THE LITTLE OLD LADY WHO WAS NOT AFRAID OF ANYTHING by Linda Williams. Crowell, 1986.

Once upon a time there was a little old lady who was not afraid of anything until one evening while walking in the woods she meets all kinds of strange things.
A great participation story!

Introducing Vocabulary
Find two words that go together and tell why.

lady	glove	herbs	basket	silver	shoes
moon	chair	cottage	afternoon	shirt	basket
scarecrow	dark	home			

Writing Activity
What could you do with a scarecrow?
You could_____
And you could_____
It would be fun to _____
And _____
This is what you could do with a scarecrow.

What can't you do with a scarecrow?
You can't _____
Or _____
You can't _____
Or _____
Because you can't do that with a scarecrow.

3. KING OF THE WOODS by David Day. Four Winds, 1993

A small wren rescues an apple from a stump guarded by a very large moose who chases all the forest animals away.

Before reading Name an animal that caws, snarls, roars, chirps, bellows.

After sharing the story use this pattern:
I saw a wren and her name was Twirp
I don't know why but she loved to chirp.

(continue with crow, wolf, bear and moose)

Find two animals alike and one different. Write sentences using this pattern:
A lion has fur.
A cat has fur.
A fish does not have fur.

4. **CAT UP A TREE** by John & Joan Hassett. Houghton, 1998.
Good introduction to community helpers. Use for **sentence expansion.**

Example Nana Quimby saw a cat up a tree.
Nana Quimby saw a purple cat up a tree.
Nice Nana Quimby saw a purple cat up a tree.
Nice Nana Quimby saw a purple cat up a tall tree.

5. **IS IT DARK, IS IT LIGHT?** by Mary Lankford. Alfred Knopf. 1991.

Introduce a concept book with mystery words. Ask a student to give a number between one and six. Read the word for that number. See if the student can guess what the book is about. If the guess is not correct, ask another student to give a number. The game continues until a student gives a correct guess or all words are read.
1. far 2. light 3. round 4. shimmer 5. glow 6. cold   **Answer**: The moon.

6. **GEORGE AND MARTHA** by James Marshall. Houghton, 1989.

List things they did in the story. Use in a "London Bridge" song.
Example   wore shoes   George and Martha looked in a mirror
                 looked in a mirror   Looked in a mirror
                 ate pea soup   Looked in a mirror,
                 went to the dentist   George and Martha looked in a mirror
                                        And wore shoes.
Working with Phonograms Write hippo riddles using words that end in **ip**.
slip trip drip dip
Riddle: What do you call a hippopotamus with a runny nose?
Answer: A drippopotamus.

7. **DAYS WITH FROG AND TOAD** by Arnold Lobel. HarperCollins, 1979.

Elaboration What could you add to Toad's bathing suit so everyone would want one like it?
Originality Pick a Story. Choose one item from each box. Add a one-sentence ending.

ONCE THERE WAS	WHO WAS	AND THEN	WRITE A ONE SENTENCE ENDING FOR YOUR STORY.
1. a talking toad	1. eating lunch	1. it began to rain	
2. a tiny girl	2. captured by a hungry giant	2. a wizard appeared	
3. a horse with wings	3. crying	3. a feather fell from a tree	
4. a spider with 100 legs	4. looking for a friend	4. a prince rode by	

ABC BOOKS FOR ALL AGES

1. ALBERT B. CUB AND ZEBRA by Ann Rockwell. Crowell, 1988.
On the **A** page Albert's friend zebra has been abducted. To find him Albert travels in an airplane and an automobile passing an accountant's sign, an Airedale and a little girl crying in anguish. How many other **A** words can you find?
  Activity Assign a different letter to teams of four.
  Each team has one day to list all the words they can find in <u>Albert B. Cub and Zebra</u> that begin with that letter. The team with the most words is the winning team OR challenge teams to see which can write the longest alliterative sentence using words from one of the letter pages. Other words can be added as needed.

2. ABC MYSTERY by Doug Cushman. Harper, 1993.
  "**A** is the art that was stolen at night. **B** is the _____ who creeps out of sight.
  C is the _____ that was left in the room. **D** is _____ Inspector McGroom."
  Solve the mystery of the missing art by following the alphabet A to Z.
  Activity Try writing an ABC advice book for students coming into your class next year.
  Brainstorm the information a new student might need.
    Example A (What are our favorite activities?) **B** (What fun books will we read?)
    C (What do we do to show we care for others?)

3. THE HOLE BY THE APPLE TREE by Nancy Polette. Greenwillow, 1991.
  An ABC fairy tale adventure where Harold and his friends meet monsters in moats, question a queen and try to save Snow White.
  Activity Brainstorm fairy tale characters that begin with each letter of the alphabet. See how many you can find in this book.
  Locate some of the tales in the school library and share them with the class.
  Use the same pattern to create a zoo adventure using animal names from A to Z.

4. GATHERING THE SUN by Alma Flor Ada. Lothrop, 1997.
  An alphabet in Spanish and English.
  Arboles: Trees, companions of my childhood.
  Activity <u>How Many Ways Can We Say Hello?</u>
  Challenge students to visit the Dewey 400 shelf in their school or public library to find foreign language picture books and discover how children all over the world greet each other.

5. TOMORROW'S ALPHABET by George Shannon. Greenwillow, 1996.
  "A is for seed, tomorrow's apple."
  "B is for egg, tomorrow's birds."
  Activity 1 Create a Tomorrow's Cook's Alphabet.
    Example F is for potatoes, tomorrow's **f**ries."

Activity 2 Take two of the words from this book and use them in this pattern:
  Eggs are just eggs until they hatch and then they become birds.
  Scraps are just scraps until they are sewn together and then they become a quilt.
Activity 3 Use the idea of <u>Tomorrow's Alphabet</u> to create Yesterday's Alphabet.
    Example A is for letter, yesterday's **a**irmail. **B** is for man. Yesterday's **b**oy.

6. <u>LOOK OUT! LETTERS ALIVE</u> by Keith Polette. Pieces of Learning, 1999.
  Activity 1 Choose any letter. Form teams. Which teams can list the most words beginning with the letter and associated with the way the letter is illustrated in a given time period?

  Activity 2 Using the words generated in Activity 1, which team can use the most words in ONE sentence to describe the letter? Other words can be added as needed.

  Activity 3 Compare two letters using this pattern:
    If I were the letter **A**
    I would artfully arise to the upper atmosphere
    And I would aerodynamically angle myself toward
    an extreme altitude
    But I wouldn't buck and balance on a bending bridge
    Because the letter **B** does that.

    If I were the letter **B**
    I would bend backwards on a breaking black bar
    And I would be the burden borne by the two below me
    But I wouldn't cling to the ceiling of a cracked cavern
    Because the letter **C** does that.

PICTURE BOOKS AND INCOGNITO TITLES

Use the dictionary to decode the words in each title in order to discover the actual title of each picture book.
  1. Procreated Uninhibited (<u>Born Free</u>)
  2. Rimy the mortal formed from white crystal precipitation
  3. Chartreuse Ova in Addition to Smoked Razorback
  4. The Minute Power Machine Professing Proficiency
  5. The Unrelenting Stannic Combatant

Now, take the title of a favorite book and expand it to ten words. (The thesaurus will help).
  Example Roller Skates by Ruth Sawyer might become: "Ball-bearing Wheels Moving Ankle High Boots Across the Floor"

Summer of the Swans would become: _____

_____

Rabbit Hill in ten words might be: _____

_____

TEACHING THINKING SKILLS WITH PICTURE BOOKS

HORTON HATCHES THE EGG by Dr. Seuss. Random House, 1968.

About the Book Horton, the elephant sits on Lazy Mayzie's egg through all kinds of hardship. When the egg is about to hatch, she returns to claim it.

A. Topic Talking To develop oral language facility partners talk from their own experience with a topic. Over a period of time, increase the amount of time and the size of the group. **Example** Three topics to introduce Horton Hatches the Egg: elephants, a circus, being responsible. (The student elaborates on a topic).

B. Topic Focusing Working in small groups, guess the answers to these questions.
1. How many pounds does an African elephant weigh? _____
2. How long is a single tusk? _____
3. How much does a single tusk weigh?_____
4. How tall is an average African elephant?_____
5. How many different kinds of elephants are there?_____
Support or deny your answers by reading the poem that follows. (Support assertions about text with evidence).

I asked my mother for a dollar,
So I could be an elephant scholar.
I measured high
I measured low
And these are figures you should know:

It's 14,000 pounds of meat,
A single tusk can be six feet
(Weighs 80 pounds) and that's not all,
This elephant is 12 feet tall.

Now Asian beasts are slightly smaller
And some from Africa much taller,
Too large to come and visit you
You'll have to see them at the zoo.

C. After Reading
   Have a debate with half the class giving reasons why Mayzie should get the egg and the other half giving reasons why Horton should get the egg. (Students take turns expressing opinions and giving reasons).

D. The student produces a response to literature that is:

Interpretative	Why do you think Horton stayed on the nest?
Analytic	How is this story like the story of Beauty and the Beast?
Evaluative	What might be a better title for this story?
Reflective	What other book character needs to read this story?

E. Recalling the story in song. Sing to "My Bonnie Lies Over the Ocean."

Verse

Oh, this is a song about (1) H_____
An (2) e_____ gentle and good,
Who promised a small (3)b_____ named (4)M_____
He'd help her if anyone could.

Chorus

(5)H_____ (6H)_____
He sat on an (7) e_____ in a tiny tree.
Horton promised
To warm the small (8) e_____ faithfully.

Verse

Through (9) a_____ he sat while the wind blew,
Then (10) w_____ came in with a roar,
In (11) s_____time his friends often teased him,
But he kept his promise once more.

Verse

Three (12) h_____ decided to catch him,
At a (13) c_____ he was on display,
That old lazy (14) b_____ (15) M_____ found him,
And wanted her (16) e_____ right away.

Verse

There then came a thumping and bumping
The (17) e_____ hatched before both their eyes,
An (18) e_____bird emerged quickly,
Which turned out to be a surprise.

AN EGG CHANT

We like eggs!
Robin's eggs

Snake eggs
Crocodile eggs
Ostrich eggs
Turtle eggs
Penguin eggs
These are just a few.

In a nest
In a hole
In the swamp
Along the dunes
In the sand
In the snow
Underground, too.

Stand and shout!
Bring them out
We like eggs!

F. Compare/Contrast Poem The student extends ideas and makes connections
to related topics.

If I were an African elephant
I would have well-developed tusks
And I'd have a rounded forehead
And two knobs at the end of my trunk
I would use my tusks to grab food and carry objects
But I wouldn't have only one knob at the end of my trunk
because an Indian elephant **has that.**

Key: 1. Horton 2. elephant 3. bird 4. Mayzie 5. Horton 6. Horton 7. egg 8. egg 9. autumn
10. winter 11. spring 12. hunters 13. circus 14. bird 15. Mayzie 16. egg 17. egg 18. elephant

TEACHING SKILLS NATURALLY FROM THE LITERATURE

THE LITTLE OLD WOMAN AND THE HUNGRY CAT by Nancy Polette. Illustrated by Frank Modell. Greenwillow, 1989.

Readers Theatre Booktalk

N1 = Narrator One N2 = Narrator Two W = Woman C = Cat

N1: One morning a little old woman baked cupcakes in real cups and then

W: went to do some errands, warning the cat to leave those cupcakes alone.

N2: But the cat

C: gobbled down the sixteen cupcakes, cups and all, and went for a walk.

N2: Before long the cat met and gobbled down

C: a one-legged man and his squealing pig, and an entire wedding party.

N1: When the little old woman came home, she saw her

W: cupcakes were missing and a cat so full it could not move.

N1: Just as she was about

W: to throw the cat outside

N2: it gobbled her down

C: sewing basket and all.

N1: The little old woman reached in her sewing basket, picked up her scissors

W: and cut a hole in that cat's side big enough to get through.

N2: Out came the one-legged man and his squealing pig.

N1: Out came the groom, the bride, the best man, the maid of honor and four fine horses prancing in a line.

W: Time for the feast!

N1: The little old woman said as she took sixteen cupcakes out of her basket.

N2: And a merrier wedding party you cannot imagine. But as for the poor cat, he had to

C: spend the whole day sewing up the hole

N1 & N2: in his side!

These strategies can be used with any picture book:

1. Higher Order Questions

A. Questions to draw logical conclusions —

   The cat probably ate the old woman because . . .

B. Questions leading to generalizations —

   You can tell from this story and other folktales you know that greedy or selfish

   characters usually end up . . .

C. Questions for evaluating (making judgements) —

   What one word in the story best describes the cat?

D. Recognizing author's point of view —

   You can tell from the story that the author views greediness with _____

E. Questions that make connections —

   Another good title for this story would be . . .

   This story reminds me of (name another story and tell why.)

2. Sing It! Recall and sequencing. (Tune: "Are You Sleeping?")

_____cat

adjective

_____cat

adjective

_____(where?)

prepositional phrase

_____(where?)

prepositional phrase

_____ and _____ (doing what?)

"ing" word   **"ing" word**

_____ and _____ (doing what?)

"ing" word   **"ing" word**

Read this book. Read this book.

Example

We Like:

Spicy   pizza   steaming   on the plate

_____   _____   _____   _____

adjective   **noun**   **"ing word"**   **prepositional phrase**

_____   _____   _____   _____

adjective   **noun**   **"ing word"**   **prepositional phrase**

Eat, little children, eat.

3. Capitalization and Punctuation Story Sequencing

Cut apart the strips. Put them in order to tell the story. Add capital letters and punctuation.

1. baked cupcakes she told her cat to
2. party he also ate the old woman who
3. one morning a little old woman
4. used her scissors to free everyone
5. a groom a bride and the whole wedding
6. them up and also ate a man his pig a
7. leave the cupcakes alone the cat ate

Key: 3,1,7,6,5,2,4

4. Recalling Plot with the "I Have, Who Has?" Game

Cut apart and distribute the cards. The person with the ** card reads the question from the card. Whoever has the answer reads it and then reads the question from his or her card.

I HAVE: He had to spend all day sewing his side. START**

WHO HAS: What did the cat eat first?

I HAVE: The cat ate cupcakes first.

WHO HAS: What else did the cat eat?

I HAVE: The cat ate a man, his pig, a wedding party and the old woman.

WHO HAS: How did everyone escape?

I HAVE: The old woman cut a hole in the cat's side.

WHO HAS: Why did the cat not attend the feast?

5. Spelling

On separate pieces of paper put the letters: **I G N P R S** Use these letters to make the following words:

A. Take three letters and make a word that tells who danced a jig. (pig)

B. Take away one letter and add two letters to tell what was in the sewing basket. Needles and ____. (pins)

C. Move the letters in pins around to tell what the old woman did with her scissors. (snip)

D. Take away one letter and add one letter to tell what she fixes. (rips)

E. Take away one letter and add two letters to tell what the bride and groom gave each other at the wedding. (rings)

F. Add one letter to tell what time of year it was. (Spring)

6. Silly Titles with Phonograms

Use the phonograms <u>OLD</u> and <u>AT</u> to create silly titles by changing the words OLD and CAT.

Example The Little Old Woman and the Hungry Bat.

PHONEMIC AWARENESS

THE NAPPING HOUSE by Don and Audrey Wood. Harcourt Brace, 1984.

This gentle story is about a snoring granny, a dreaming child, a dozing dog, a snoozing cat, and a slumbering mouse, all on one cozy bed. But wait! When a wakeful flea arrives to join the rest there is a surprise in store and no one is sleeping anymore.

1. Phoneme Isolation Song
("Three Blind Mice")
Who's asleep?
Who's asleep?
Can you tell?
Can You tell?
The sleeper's name begins with **G**
Now who do you think that it could be?
Granny, Dog, Flea?
Granny, Dog, Flea.

2. Rhyming Song
("For He's A Jolly Good Fellow")
Who's asleep on the big bed?
Who's asleep on the big bed?
Who's asleep on the big bed?
It's a word that rhymes with **log**.

Repeat with   wild/child; sat/cat;
                mouse/house

3. Rhyming Song
("Clementine")
Say some words that
Rhyme with **FLEA** and
Write them on the line below
_____ and _____ rhyme with **FLEA**
These are rhyming words we know.

4. Phoneme Blending Song
("Oh Where, Oh Where Has
My Little Dog Gone?")
Now who's asleep in the Napping House?
Yes, who's asleep in the bed?
It starts with **D** and ends with **OG**
The _____ is asleep in the bed. (DOG)

Add more verses:
Starts with M and ends with OUSE
Starts with F and ends with LEA
Starts with C and ends with AT

5. Phoneme Isolation Song
("Old MacDonald")
D is the sound that starts these words
Dog, Doze, Dream
With a D/D / here and a D/D/ there
Here a /D/, there a /D/
Everywhere a /D/D/
D is the sound that starts these words
Dog, Doze, Dreaming.

Add verses: Big, Bad, Bed for B
Mice, Mouse, Moose for M

6. Substitution Song
("If You're Happy And You
Know It")
If you change the **C** in cat to a **B**
If you change the **C** in cat to a **B**
If you change the **C** to **B**
Then a **Cat** becomes a **Bat**
If you change the **C** in **Cat** to a **B**.

If you change **CH** in child to an **M**
If you change **CH** in child to an **M**
If you change **CH** to **M**
Then a **child** becomes most **Mild**
If you change **CH** in **child** to an **M**.

Add verses:

Change the **D** in **Dog** to an **L**
Change the **M** in **mouse** to an **H**

HOW SENTENCES WORK

Joseph Had A Little Overcoat by Simms Taback. Viking, 1999.

Joseph had a little overcoat. It got old and worn so he made a jacket out of it and went to the fair.

1. Vocabulary substitution
Joseph had a little overcoat.

Suppose we didn't want to use the word **overcoat**. What other words could we use instead? Suggestions will begin to flow.
Joseph had a little overcoat.
                    monkey
Suppose we didn't want to use the word **little**. What other word could we use instead?
Joseph had a little   overcoat.
                    purple   monkey
Suppose we didn't want to use the word **had**? Who else has a different word?
Joseph   had   a   little   overcoat.
              wore   purple   monkey.
If we add /**The**/ as the first word of the sentence, what word could we use in place of **Joseph**?

Joseph	had	a	little	monkey.
The bear	wore	a	purple	overcoat.

2. Expanding Sentences

Joseph made a jacket from his overcoat.

What describing words can we put in front of jacket?
Joseph made a   jacket from his overcoat.
            new
            fancy
What describing words could we put in front of overcoat?

Joseph made a   jacket from his   overcoat.
            new   **tattered**
            fancy   **old**
There is one other way to make the sentence longer. Let's add a whole collection of words that belong together.

Joseph made a   jacket from his   overcoat.
            new   **tattered**
            fancy   **old**

and wore it to the fair.
and went to visit his sister.
and drank a glass of hot tea.

How many words can you remove from this sentence and still have a correct sentence?
How many different short sentences can you make?
Joseph had an overcoat that was old and worn
so he made a jacket out of it and went to the fair.

PICTURE BOOKS AND PRODUCTIVE THINKING

"The present belongs to the sober, the cautious, the routine-prone. But the future belongs to those who do not rein in their imaginations." Kornei Chukovsky

FLUENCY Brainstorming many responses.

1. Name many **B** words associated with the **B** page in Keith Polette's Look Out, Letters Alive. Pieces of Learning 1999.
2. Brainstorm words to describe a toad.
   See Toad by Ruth Brown. Dutton, 1997.
   What additional words did the author use that you did not?
3. Albert B. Cub and Zebra by Rockwell, Ann. Crowell, 1977.
   Find dozens of pictures beginning with the same letter!

FLEXIBILITY Finding new categories; stretching the mind beyond the expected response.

1. So Many Dynamos by Jon Agee. Farrar, 1993. Palindromes galore!
The title reads the same backward and forward.
2. Elvis Lives by Jon Agee. Farrar, 2000.
The same letters are used in both words, Elvis and lives.
3. A Surfeit of Similes by Norton Juster. Morow, 1989.
Original and clever collection of similes."As harsh as a snub."

ORIGINALITY Responding in new ways.

1. Workshop by Andrew Clements. Clarion, 1999.
Creative personification of workshop tools. "Axe is the great divider."
2. Life Is No Fair by Stephen Mane. Unusual solutions to problems.

ELABORATION Adding to a product to enhance it or make it more complete or original.

1. See William Wegman's Mother Goose. Note how he elaborates using dogs as characters.
2. What could you add to Toad's bathing suit so every animal would want one like it?
See Frog and Toad All Year by Arnold Lobel.
3. What could little pig add to the straw house so wolf could not blow it down?
4. See books by Larry Shles: Hoots and Toots and Hairy Brutes, Moths and Mothers, Feathers and Fathers, Aliens in My Nest, Nose Drops. Squib Publications, 1991.
Both visual and verbal elaboration.

FUN WRITING PATTERNS

1. The girl in <u>My Brown Bear Barney</u> always takes things with her when she goes someplace. When she goes to bed, she takes "a good book or two, our old dog Charlie, an apple for the morning, a big silver flashlight and her brown bear Barney."

What do each of these things tell you about her?

She takes a book because _____.

She takes a flashlight because _____.

She takes her dog because _____.

Try the pattern with your favorite book characters.

When _____ went to _____, he or she took

_____, _____, _____, and

_____.

When the little pig went to market he took . . .

When Red Riding Hood went through the woods she took . . .

When Cinderella went to the ball she took . . .

2. **Days of the Week Story**

Cookie the cat made a lot of messes in the story <u>Cookie's Week</u> by Cindy Ward. Scholastic, 1988.

What caused water to get on the floor? How did Cookie get dirt on the carpet? How did garbage get on the kitchen floor?

Suppose Cookie jumped inside of a first grader's book bag on Sunday night. The next day he rode to school! What kinds of messes could Cookie make at school?

On Monday Cookie _____.

There was _____ everywhere!

On Tuesday Cookie _____.

There was _____ everywhere!

On Wednesday Cookie _____.

There was _____ everywhere!

On Thursday Cookie _____.

There was _____ everywhere!

Tomorrow is Friday. Maybe Cookie will _____.

IMOGENE'S ANTLERS by David Small. Crown, 1985.

Imogene woke up with antlers. Her mother fainted. Imogene had trouble getting dressed, going through a door and coming down the stairs. The doctor could find nothing wrong. The school principal had no advice. Her brother said she was a miniature elk. Again her mother fainted. The antlers made a great towel dryer, bird feeder and doughnut dispenser. When the milliner designed a hat to cover the antlers everyone cheered. Her mother fainted. But the next morning Imogene found the antlers had disappeared. In their place were . . .

ACTIVITY WRITING PATTERN Follow the pattern to write another Imogene story.

When Imogene woke up she discovered she had _____

Tell how a character reacted_____

The _____ did cause Imogene some problems. (Name 2)

_____

_____

There did not seem to be any help for Imogene. (Tell how two characters were not able to help)

_____

_____

But the good things about Imogene's _____ were (Name 2)

_____

_____

The next morning when Imogene woke up her _____

had disappeared, but instead Imogene discovered _____

PICTURE BOOKS AND BEGINNING RESEARCH

DEAR MR. BLUEBERRY by Simon James. Margaret K. McElderry Books, 1992.

A little girl finds a whale in her wading pool. She writes to her teacher, Mr. Blueberry, for information about whales. As children listen to this or any other text that has information about whales, they add additional items to the data bank. When the data bank is complete, the information is used in the patterns below.

Add more items to the **Whale Data Bank**.

Lives	**Eats**	**Has**
Ocean	fish	flippers
salt water	plankton	blubber
_____	_____	_____
_____	_____	_____

What It Does
breathes air
does tricks

_____

Use the information from the data bank in one of these patterns:

A. London Bridge

Big blue whales have _____ and _____
_____ and _____
_____ and _____
Big blue whales eat _____ and _____
And they _____

B. If I Were Pattern

Name the thing you want to be
Tell where it is found
Name one thing it can do for someone
Name a second thing it can do
Repeat the first line.

C. Write A Whale Story

Some _____ have their own _____

where they_____.

Sometimes they go around_____

or sometimes they just _____.

But to this very day, some _____

have their own _____

ACTIVITIES WITH THE CORETTA SCOTT KING

AWARD WINNING PICTURE BOOKS

The Coretta Scott King Award is given annually by the Social Responsibilities Round Table of the American Library Association to an African-American author and an African-American illustrator for outstanding inspirational and educational contributions to literature for children.

AFRICA DREAM by Eloise Greenfield. Illustrated by Carole Byard. John Day Co., 1977. 1978 Winner

A young child dreams of visiting long ago Africa, crossing an ocean in "one smooth jump." The animals are waiting, elephants, zebras, and camels. The child visits a market place and sees ancient civilizations with their tall stone buildings.

Pre Reading Activity Topic Talking Partner A speaks to Partner B on a topic given by the leader for five seconds. The leader says"switch" and B speaks to A until the leader says "stop." The second round is ten seconds and the third round is fifteen seconds. Topics are related to the selection to be read.

Topic Focusing Work with a small group to guess the answers to these questions. Total all the numbers. Then listen to the poem to support or deny guesses.

1. How many counties are there in Africa? _____
2. How many miles is it from north to south in Africa? _____
3. What percent of Africa is jungle? _____
4. What percent of land in Africa can be farmed? _____
5. What is the most common African animal? _____
       Total your number answers for 1- 4 _____

Africa Poem (Answers to Africa quiz)

> The number of African countries you see
> Numbers right at fifty-three
> It's 5000 miles from north to south
> Where the Nile River has its mouth.
> One fourth is jungle where wild birds cry
> The rest is desert, hot and dry.
> Only six per cent of the land is tilled
> Not enough to keep food baskets filled.
> A land with many animals blessed
> The most common one is never guessed.
> The camel wins, for it survives
> In deserts where it lives and thrives.

AIDA told by Leontyne Price. Illustrated by Leo and Diane Dillon. Harcourt Brace, 1990. 1991 Winner

Aida is a princess, captured and brought to Egypt as a slave. A tragic love affair sees both Aida and the man she loves put to death.

ABOUT THE OPERA "AIDA"

Activity Giuseppe Verdi wrote the music for the opera and when a man named Prospero Bertani went to listen to Aida at Reggio Emilia, Italy, he was not satisfied with it. He wrote Verdi asking to be reimbursed for expenses. Do you think Verdi should pay the man who did not like his opera? Give reasons he should and should not.

Activity A Karaoke Book Report

Sung to the Grand March from the opera Aida

A tale, told of a brave princess
of Ethiopia
Captured as a slave
Servant to
Egypt's Queen
Oh, the poor girl.

And then, the girl she fell in love
She loved a captain bold
And he loved her, too
Loved her, too
Love so true,
Oh, the poor man

Oh, it was jealousy,
yes, it was jealousy
Led to betrayal and a trial, too.

Yes, Death was the sad fate they met
Imprisoned in the vault
Jealousy at fault.
Sad ending
Bad ending
Of this old tale.

BEAT THE STORY-DRUM, PUM-PUM by Ashley Bryan. Simon & Schuster. 1980.

Five Nigerian folktales retold in language as rhythmic as the beat of a story-drum.

Activity Choose an animal from this story to read about. List four clues about the animal. One must be a "give away" clue. Ask a member of your class to give you a number between one and four. Read the clue for that number. The student can guess or pass. The game continues until the animal name is guessed or all clues have been read.

CHRISTMAS IN THE BIG HOUSE, CHRISTMAS IN THE QUARTERS by Patricia and Frederick McKissack. Scholastic, 1994. 1995 Winner

It is Christmastime on a plantation in Virginia. The year is 1859. The Big House is awash with light and color and elegance. In the slave Quarters nearby, there is no such grandeur for the families who live in cramped quarters with dirt floors.

Activity Write a Compare Contrast poem book report
  Example
  If I lived in the Big House
  I would find many presents under the tree
  And sing by the Yule log
  And eat roast turkey with trimmings
  And go to sleep under a down comforter
  But I wouldn't wake up to no tree and no gifts
  And sing sad songs
  And eat fat and greens
  And work from morning until night
  Because the slaves in the Quarters do that

CORNROWS by Camille Yarbrough. Illustrated by Carole Byard. Coward-McCann, 1979. 1980 winner
  Two children watch their Great Grandmaw braid their mother's hair and learn the meaning of many cornrow styles. She tells of African symbols of courage, honor, wisdom, love and strength. Then she tells of the slavers who came and put the people in chains, but the spirit of the symbols lives on in the accomplishments of many African Americans.

Activity Substitute one of the qualities Great Grandma told about for "dreams" in this Langston Hughes poem.

> Hold fast to **dreams**
> For if **dreams die**,
> Life is a **broken-winged bird**
> **That cannot fly**.

  Example
> Hold fast to **courage**
> For if **courage disappears**
> Life is a **horror show**
> **Filled with constant fears.**

THE CREATION by James Weldon Johnson. Illustrated by James E. Ransame. Holiday House, 1994. 1995 Winner
  The story of God's creation of the world beginning with the sun, the moon and the stars.

Activity A Wish Book
Choose one or more of the creatures God created and give it a wish. Illustrate the creature and the wish.
  Example Snails wish for roller skates so that they could move faster.

Trees wish for _____

The stars wish for _____

Grass wishes for _____

Giraffes wish for _____

THE DARK THIRTY: SOUTHERN TALES OF THE SUPERNATURAL by Patricia
McKissack. Illustrated by Brian Pinkney. Knopf, 1992. 1993 Winner

Here is a collection of ten hair-raising tales rooted in African-American history and the oral storytelling tradition. Each is memorable and each lets the reader experience the delicious horror of a tale of the dark thirty.

Activity Writing About Scary Things
Complete these sentences.
1. Walking in a dark woods is scary but _____ is terrifying.
2. Being the victim of a voodoo doll is scary but _____ is terrifying.
3. Seeing cloudy windows no one else sees is scary but _____ is terrifying.
4. A train coming right at you is scary but _____ is terrifying.
5. Being able to see the future is scary but _____ is terrifying.
6. Going into a dark house alone at night is scary but _____ is terrifying.

HALF A MOON AND ONE WHOLE STAR by Crescent Dragonwagon. Illustrated by
Jerry Pinkney. Macmillan, 1986. 1987 Winner

A young child sleeps, peacefully unaware of the night activity that surrounds her. Robins, parrots and chickens sleep while owls, bats, possums and raccoons awaken to begin their nightly outings. In the city Johnny gets ready to play his saxophone at the club, bakers are busy at their ovens, while ships at the dock weigh anchor and start their journeys. As the night ends, the possums and owls get ready for sleep.

Activity Turn On the Night
What might you see around your house or yard if you could turn on the night? Add things from your list to this poem.

Turn on the night and in the moonlight
We'll see

_____ and _____ and _____
Turn off the night and in the daylight
We'll see

_____ and _____ and _____

HER STORIES: AMERICAN FOLKTALES, FAIRY TALES AND TRUE TALES by
Virginia Hamilton. Illustrated by Leo and Diane Dillon. Scholastic, 1995. 1996 Winner

The nineteen stories in this collection focus on the magical lore of African-American women. They range from light-hearted trickster tales to tales of enchanted worlds. "Catskinella" is a Cinderella tale of a poor girl whose father wants her to marry a woodsman. She does not like the man and asks for help from her godmother. On her wedding day she runs away in her catskin dress, taking the ring with her. She finds work in the castle and puts the ring in a cake for the prince. When he finds the ring he is determined to find its owner and make her his bride.

Activity Cinderella tales come from every time and culture in the world. Think of a time or place to set your Cinderella tale. Be sure that you add items in the story that reflect the place, culture or historical era you are writing about. You will need to research the time or place before writing.

MINTY: A STORY OF YOUNG HARRIET TUBMAN by Alan Schroeder. Illustrated by Jerry Pinkney. Dial, 1996. 1997 Winner
   Young Harriet Tubman was stubborn and headstrong. She longed and prepared for only one thing . . . to be free!

Activity Create a Mystery Report about a famous African-American woman.
List eight facts (or clues) about the person. Mix up the clues. One must be a "give away" clue. Ask a volunteer to give a number between 1 and 8. Read the clue for that number. The person can guess or pass. Ask for more volunteers until all clues are read or the topic is guessed.

   1. I had sixteen brothers and sisters.
   2. I was the first child in my family not born a slave.
   3. I served as an advisor to President Roosevelt.
   4. I attended a mission school, a seminary and a Bible Institute.
   5. I was named "Mother of the Century" in 1954.
   6. I was a college president.
   7. I opened a first school for Negro children in 1904.
   8. I served as a U.S. representative to the United Nations.
(Answer: Mary McLeod Bethune)

MIRANDY AND BROTHER WIND by Patricia C. McKissack. Illustrated by Jerry Pinkney. Knopf, 1988. 1989 Winner
   Mirandy tries to catch the wind to be her partner in the cakewalk with no success. Her partner turns out to be more than she expected.

Activity Everyone brought something good to eat to the dance. What do you hope they brought? Complete the song and sing to "Skip To My Lou"

| _____ | chicken | _____ | _____ |
| adjective | noun | "ing" word | prepositional phrase |

| _____ | _____ | _____ | _____ |
| adjective | noun | "ing" word | prepositional phrase |

| _____ | _____ | _____ | _____ |
| adjective | noun | "ing" word | prepositional phrase |

Eat, all you dancers, eat!

MUFARO'S BEAUTIFUL DAUGHTERS: AN AFRICAN TALE by John Steptoe. Lothrop, 1987. 1988 Winner

Long ago in Africa, Mufaro had two beautiful daughters. Manyara was selfish and greedy and teased her sister Nyasha, who was kind and loving. Manyara spent her days in a bad temper. Nyasha spent her days tending her garden and singing to her friend, the little garden snake who lived there. When both daughters were to go to the city to see the king, only one, because of her kindness to others becomes his bride.

Activity Compare the two girls using this pattern.

If I were Nyasha I would _____

And I'd _____

And _____

But I wouldn't _____
Because Manyara does that.

If I visited Africa I would see _____

And _____

And _____

But I wouldn't see _____

Because I'd see that in _____

NATHANIEL TALKING by Eloise Greenfield. Illustrated by Jan Spivey Gilchrist. Black Butterfly Children's Press. 1988. Honor

Nathaniel B. Free is a spunky, spirited nine-year-old poet who raps and rhymes about his world, from what it's like to be nine, to his education, missing his mama, making friends, misbehaving, his daddy, his aunt and his future. Along with a fine intellect, Nathaniel is playful, curious and enthusiastic and he shares with candor his thoughts about the world and his place in it.

Activity Yesterday, Today and Tomorrow
Write about yourself to complete this pattern.

Nathaniel might write:
Yesterday was walking all over the neighborhood with friends.
Today is a girl puffing out her cheeks and making a funny face.
Tomorrow is being president of the United States.

THE PATCHWORK QUILT by Valerie Flourney. Illustrated by Jerry Pinkney. Dial, 1985. 1986 Winner

Tanya's Grandma liked to sit in her favorite chair by the window where the light shone in. She needed good light to work on her patchwork quilt, made from bits and pieces of her children's and grandchildren's lives.

Activity Use the pattern that follows to write about things that change from one form to another.

Scraps are just scraps until they are sewn together and then they become a quilt.

A shirt is just a shirt until . . .

A potato is just a potato until . . .

A tree is just a tree until . . .

A nail is just a nail until . . .

What others can you add?

THE PEOPLE COULD FLY by Virginia Hamilton. Illustrated by Leo and Diane Dillon. Knopf, 1985. 1986 Winner

Here is a collection of tales that represent the best of black folklore. The People Could Fly is a fantasy escape tale of slaves who worked in the fields from sun up till sun down. Some, however, were able to rise above the fields in a flight to freedom.

Activity In the story The People Could Fly there were many feelings expressed – sadness, anger, despair, joy. Write about the feeling as if it were alive. Follow this pattern

I am (name the feeling) _____

I am surrounded by _____

I cannot escape _____

I live with _____

I spend my days _____

My cousins are _____

My clothing is _____

I give to those I touch _____

I am (repeat the first line)_____

TAR BEACH by Faith Ringold. Crown, 1991. 1992 Winner

Eight-year-old Cassie lives in New York City in Harlem where she lets her imagination soar as the family spends summer evenings on the roof top of their apartment building.

Activity Create a Big City Tall Tale

First, think of a word for each of the 15 listed items (Use the name, Cassie, for items 5, 7, and 14) Name: 1. a size 2. a color 3. an animal 4. a place to sleep 5. Cassie 6. way to travel 7. Cassie 8. something to read 9. same as #3 10. animal noise 11. animal (not #3) 12. animal 13. animal 14. Cassie 15. same as #6.

Substitute the words above for the numbers in the story that follows.

Beside the Brooklyn Bridge there was a (1) (2) (3) who was sound asleep on a (4). (5) approached on a (6). (7) was reading a (8) and stumbled over the (9) who awakened and gave a loud (10) that frightened the other river creatures including the (11), (12) and (13). (14) left quickly on (15) vowing never to disturb the river animals again.

NANCY'S ALL TIME FAVORITE PICTURE BOOKS

ANNIE AND THE WILD ANIMALS by Jan Brett. Houghton Mifflin Company, 1985.
   It had been a long winter and the snow was falling. Annie could not find Taffy anywhere. Annie waited and waited but her cat did not return so Annie decided to make some corn cakes and leave them at the edge of the woods to attract another small animal to be her pet. She could not believe it when a moose, a wildcat, a bear and a stag appeared. What will Annie do? Will she ever see Taffy again?
Pre Reading Activity Suppose that your family was ready to sit down to lunch when the doorbell rings and four friends come to visit. You have just enough food on the table for your family. Working in groups of four, rank order what you would do first, second, third and last.
1. Add more water to the soup, cut the sandwiches in half and ask the visitors to join you.
2. Don't answer the door.
3. Go to the store and get more food.
4. Ask the visitors to wait while the family has lunch.

ASHPET An Appalachian Tale retold by Joanne Compton. Holiday House, 1994.
   Long ago in a cabin by Eagle's Nest Mountain lived a servant girl called Ashpet. All day long she chopped firewood, washed clothes, and cooked and cleaned for the Widow Hooper and her cranky daughters. Ashpet had so much work to do, the widow wouldn't even allow her to go to the church picnic. Ashpet's life changes for the better, however, when old Granny shows up and works some magic. How Ashpet outshines the widow's daughters and captures the heart of the doctor's son makes a delightful and surprising tale.
Activity Create a Cinderella tale from another time or place. Follow the pattern in Ashpet.

THE BEAR CAME OVER TO MY HOUSE by Rick Walton. Putnam, 2001.
   "The bear came over to my house to see what he could **see**. And what do you think he saw? ME!"
Activity Use as a fun writing pattern. (do, bring, get, seek, wake)

THE BOSTON TEA PARTY by Pamela Edwards Putnam, 2001. Retold using the "House that Jack Built" pattern.
   "These are the leaves that grew from a bush in a far off land and became part of the Boston Tea Party. This is the tea that was made from the leaves . . ."
Activity Use as a model for reporting on a historical incident.
   Example "These are the trees that grew in the woods that became part of the Constitution. This is the paper made from the trees . . ."

THE BUNYIP OF BERKELEY'S CREEK by Jenny Wagner. Puffin Books, 1973.
   A Bunyip wants to know what he looks like but does not receive a satisfactory answer from the platypus, wallaby or emu. A man tells him that "Bunyips simply don't exist." The sad Bunyip wanders off and finds a most unexpected surprise.
Activity Look at the Bunyip on the cover of the book. Brainstorm: What could we do to beautify a Bunyip?

THE CAKE THAT MACK ATE by Rose Robart. Little Brown, 1986.
   A cumulative story about all it took to put together a cake for Mack's birthday. Mack turns out to be a dog.
Pre Reading Activity Let children guess yes or no whether or not these words will be in a birthday story. Listen to support or deny guesses. Hen, egg, corn, seed, woman, farmer, candles, cake.

THE CELLO OF MR. O by Jane Cutler. E.P. Dutton, 1999.
   An old man plays his cello to soothe the people of a city torn by war.
Activity Research the war in Bosnia or Afghanistan. Write a recipe for a city under siege.
   Example
      Take a large measure of extreme shortages
      Mix in hunger and cold
      Add bitter and heavy fighting
      With 16 large Yugoslav army tanks
      Decorate with orange flash of mortars
      Sprinkle with streets littered with bricks and broken glass
      Add Muslims, Serbs and Croats
      Remove hope of escape
      Place Bosnia under siege for four years
      Serve with grief and tears.

CHRYSANTHEMUM by Kevin Henkes, Greenwillow, 1991.
   Chrysanthemum loved her name until she went to school. The children laughed because her name was so long and she was named after a flower. The teasing continued until they discovered the name of their favorite music teacher!
Activity Write a class poem about a seed or a flower.
Use the "If I Were" pattern. Name the flower. Tell where it is found. Name two things it can do. Repeat the first line.
   Example
      If I were a flower seed
      Snug in the ground
      I would push myself up
      Lift my face to the sun and bloom
      If I were a flower seed

CLICK, CLACK, MOO COWS THAT TYPE by Doreen Cronin. Simon & Schuster, 2000.
   Farmer Brown has a problem. His cows like to type. All day long he hears click, clack, moo, click, clack moo. But Farmer Brown's problems really begin when his cows start leaving him notes. They demand electric blankets because the barn is cold at night. Not only do they demand the blankets, but they refuse to give milk until they receive them.
Activity Summarize the story using this pattern:
Here is how the cows got electric blankets.

First _____

Then _____

Finally _____

DAYS WITH FROG AND TOAD by Arnold Lobel. Harper, 1979.
   One of a series of "I Can Read" books about the gentle friendship of Frog and Toad.
Activity What could you add to Toad's bathing suit so that the animals who made fun of it would want one like it? How can Frog get Toad out of bed by using one of these items? A feather, popcorn, a book, a drum, a pan of water?

THE DIGGERS by Margaret Wise Brown. Hyperion, 1995.
   A beautiful example of the writer's craft! Repetition, personification and rich language that children rarely hear on television. The child listens in awe as small animals create their homes and huge machines create tunnels, bridges and great cities.
Pre Reading Activity List all the reasons you can think of to dig a hole. Then listen to see if you can add to your list.

DINORELLA by Pamela Duncan Edwards. Hyperion, 1997.
   Dinorella is dying to go to the dance, but her dreadful stepsisters, Dora and Doris, declare she's too dowdy and dull, so Dinorella is stuck in the den doing dishes. Then Fairydactyl arrives and bedecks Dinorella with some dazzling diamonds. to save the Duke and the day.
Activity Write alliterative sentences about fairy tale characters.
   Example Rumplestiltskin raved and ranted before he was routed.

THE DOORBELL RANG by Pat Hutchins. Mulberry Books, 1986.
   Each ring of the doorbell brings more and more friends to share a dozen delicious cookies. But when twelve hungry children are already seated at the table and the doorbell rings again, how can everyone get a fair share?
Activity Let children share ideas about what to do when the doorbell rings for the last time. Then finish the story for a most satisfactory ending.

FLOSSIE AND THE FOX by Patricia McKissack. Dial, 1986.
   Flossie lives with Big Mama in the Piney Woods. One morning Big Mama asks Flossie to take a basket of eggs to Miss Viola at the farm on the other side of the woods. On the way Flossie meets the fox (who loves eggs.) In order to get through the woods safely and with all the eggs in her basket, Flossie fools the fox into believing that she doesn't know what kind of creature he is.
Activity Compare this tale to Little Red Riding Hood. How are the two stories alike and different?

FORTUNATELY by Remy Charlip. Aladdin Books, 1983.
   Fortunately Ned was invited to a surprise party. Unfortunately the party was a thousand miles away. Everything seems to go wrong for Ned as his luck turns from good to bad to good again.
Activity Use as a writing model, reporting the fortunate and unfortunate events that might happen on the way to school.

FROM A DISTANCE by Julie Gold. Dutton, 2000.
   An illustrated picture book of the song. Play the Bette Midler recording.
Activity Write a protest song about something that needs attention in your community. Be sure your facts are correct.

GEORGE AND MARTHA by James Marshall. Houghton-Mifflin, 1972.
   Humorous tales of good friends who find joy in small everyday occurrences.
Activity List phrases from the story that tell what they did together:
   Example Look in a mirror, go to the dentist, wear shoes. Use the phrases in a "London Bridge" song.

GOOSE by Molly Bang. Blue Sky/Scholastic. 1996.
   The story of a little goose who had to leave home to find what no one could teach her.
Activity Read aloud to soft background music. Ask children what the story means to them.

HECKEDY PEG by Audrey Wood. Harcourt-Brace, 1987.
   Seven children named for the days of the week meet a witch who turns them into food. The mother can save them if she can guess which food each child has become. The mother tries to match each child with a gift the child had asked for. Monday wanted butter. Tuesday wanted a knife. Wednesday asked for a pitcher. Thursday wanted honey. Friday wanted salt. Saturday asked for crackers and Sunday wanted egg pudding.
Activity Help the mother match each child's wish with the seven foods on the table: bread, pie, fish, milk, porridge, cheese and roast rib.

HOOTS AND TOOTS AND HAIRY BRUTES by Larry Shles. Squib Publications, 1990.
   Squib is a small owl who cannot hoot but saves the day when his parents are threatened.
Activity Students make a sketch of Squib and elaborate on their sketches to show what he might become – a firefighter? a scuba diver? President?

A HOUSE IS A HOUSE FOR ME by Mary Ann Hoberman. Viking, 1978.
   Poetry that names many kinds of houses. A kennel is a house for a dog. A box is a house for some crackers. A dog is a house for a flea.
Activity How many more houses can children name?

IF I WERE IN CHARGE OF THE WORLD by Judith Viorst. Aladdin Books, 1981.
   If you've ever had trouble apologizing or keeping a secret, had a crush or a broken heart, there's a poem here for you.
Activity The title poem makes a great writing model.
If I were in charge of_____
There would be _____ You wouldn't have _____
I'd cancel_____ But the greatest thing I would do is_____.

IRON HORSES by Verla Kay. Putnams, 1999
   Fast moving poetry that describes the building of the Transcontinental Railroad.
Activity Use the poetry model to write about another event in history.

THE IMPORTANT BOOK by Margaret Wise Brown. Harper, 1949.
   The author begins describing a series of everyday things by saying "The important thing about _____ is . . ." Details are added and the first sentence is repeated.
Activity An excellent model for teaching paragraph writing. Each child can write about something important to him or her.

KAT KONG by Dave Pilkey. Harcourt, 1993.

   A group of explorers led by Captain Limburger captures Kat Kong and brings him to Mouseopolis. The creature escapes and climbs the Romano Inn with Rosie, the mouse, in his clutches. Captain Limburger devises a plan to rescue Rosie. At the end it is "curiosity that kills the cat."

Activity Introduce the cliché. Challenge students to find as many as they can in the story. Compare the story with the movie "King Kong."

THE KING WHO RAINED by Fred Gwynne. Simon & Schuster, 1970.

   Homophones introduced in a clever way with fun illustrations.

KOALA LOU by Mem Fox. Illustrated by Pamela Lofts. Harcourt, 1988.

   There was once a baby koala so soft and round that all who saw her loved her. One hundred times a day her mother would say, "Koala Lou, I do love you." Years passed and brothers and sisters were born. Soon mother was so busy she didn't have time to tell Koala Lou that she loved her. Koala Lou longed for her mother's attention once again. How could she get it?

IDEAS	Fast	Safe	Possible	Will work	Total

Score 1=no 2=maybe 3=yes

LILLY'S PURPLE PLASTIC PURSE by Kevin Henkes. Greenwillow, 1998.

   School was a wonderful place to be until the day Lilly took her new glittery glasses and purple plastic purse to school. She was so anxious to share her new things that she ignored her teacher's warning to wait and interrupted the class. When her teacher took the things to keep for her until the end of the day, Lilly was furious. She drew a terrible picture of Mr. Slinger and put it into his book bag. Can you guess what will happen next?

A Writing Pattern

Lilly thought of many things she wanted to be when she grew up:
a dancer, a surgeon, an ambulance driver, a diva, a pilot and a scuba diver.
Choose one of Lilly's ideas and write about it using this pattern

   I wish I were a diva (tell what)

   Standing on an opera stage (tell where)

   Singing a beautiful song (doing what)

   Hitting high notes with the orchestra (tell how)

THE MICROSCOPE by Maxine Kumin. Harper, 1984.

   A poem that re-creates 17th century Holland and the fascinating world revealed by Aton Leewenhoek's microscope.

Activity An excellent writing model for older students to use in reporting on the life and work of a famous person.

THE MIGHTIEST by Keiko Kasza. Putnam, 2001.

A bear, lion and elephant find a golden crown in the forest. The mightiest will get to keep the crown. When a tiny old woman comes along, they take turns seeing who can scare her the most. Then along comes a bully but the tiny old woman turns out to be the mightiest of all.

Activity Class members write short sentences on separate pieces of paper. Two students act a scene where the tiny woman takes George home and talks to him about being a bully. Each, in turn, picks up a sentence and must use it in the improvisation. The scene ends when each has used three sentence strips.

MY LOVE FOR YOU by Susan L. Roth. Dial, 1997.

How do tiny animals measure their love? A mouse's love is bigger than one bear, taller than two giraffes . . .

Activity Children can add other animal phrases up to ten or beyond.

THE MYSTERIES OF HARRIS BURDICK by Chris Van Allsburg. Houghton-Mifflin, 1984.

An artist leaves fourteen strange drawings with puzzling captions. It is up to the reader to put together the story behind each.

Activity Fourteen excellent writing prompts for older students.

NOSE DROPS by Larry Shles. Squib Publications, 1994.

Geoffrey is a nose who has lost his face. He will never become a famous scientist like Doctor Hypotenose or a great leader like Julius Sneezer. Filled with visual and verbal puns, this nose is sure to please.

Activity Note how the artist elaborates on a nose to turn it into different figures. Outline your hand on a large sheet of paper. How can you elaborate on it to turn it into something else?

POTLUCK by Anne Shelby. Orchard, 1991.

A good introduction to alliteration as each child brings food to a feast that begins with the first letter of his or her name.
"Christine came with carrot cake and corn on the cob. Don did dumplings."

Activity Let children use their own names in telling what they will bring to a feast. Each child's sentence can be illustrated and pages placed in a class book.

RIDDLE CITY USA! by Marco and Giulio Maestro. HarperCollins, 1994.

A book of geography riddles. "How do kings and queens dine in North Dakota? With grand forks."

Activity Students will have fun guessing the answers to the riddles and learning about geography at the same time.

SNOW WHITE IN NEW YORK by Fiona French. Oxford University Press, 1986.

A wicked stepmother sends her bodyguard to shoot Snow White but he leaves her in the dark streets alone. She becomes the singer in a jazz club and is cared for by seven jazz musicians until the stepmother finds her once again.

Activity Acrostic summary. Summarize the tale using each letter of the title as the beginning of a sentence.

SO YOU WANT TO BE PRESIDENT? by Judith St. George. Philomel, 2000.

Comparisons in many ways of the lives of 41 presidents from their previous occupations to their pets, education and dress.

Activity Use as a research model. Select six famous people who have the same occupation and compare them by names, birthplace, size, family, looks, pets, music or art ability, education or other attributes.

TERRIBLE THINGS by Eve Bunting. HarperCollins, 1989.

An allegory on the Holocaust.

Activity Write about the holocaust using the "Just for a Day" pattern from Joanne Ryder's <u>White Bear, Ice Bear</u>

One _____ morning your room is _____ and _____. Outside your window you hear_____, calling you, changing you until you realize that you are a _____ and live in _____. A _____ hangs around your neck. You are a _____ now. By day you _____. By night you are _____. Silently you _____ and wonder _____. But wait! You hear a _____ approaching. Now you sense a familiar _____. You walk toward _____ and feel _____ changing you. You step through the _____ and run inside. Hungry and happy to be home again and _____.

THE WOLF'S CHICKEN STEW by Keiko Kasza. Putnam's, 1987.

A hungry wolf takes goodies to Mrs. Chicken's house to fatten her up for his stew. He finds, however, that her chicks are too much for him to handle and he bakes cookies for them instead.

Activity In groups of four each child lists two of his or her favorite foods. The group must then rank order the eight foods from the one the group likes best to least.

YIKES by Alison Lester. Houghton-Mifflin, 1995.

Captain Salty Scott can't control his sinking ship. A circus star loses hold of his swing. In seven hair raising adventures the reader chooses who he or she will be before the outcome of the adventure is revealed.

Activity Encourage children to choose who they will be as each character is introduced, then find out which one survives the adventure.

THE Z WAS ZAPPED by Chris Van Allsburg. Houghton-Mifflin, 1987.

The **B** was badly bitten and the **C** was cut to ribbons. Twenty-six alphabet adventures with appropriate illustrations.

Activity Take any one letter and brainstorm all the words beginning with that letter that are associated with the way the letter is illustrated.

FAIRY TALES, FOLKTALES AND FANTASY

Fairy tales and fantasy can create a startling new environment for the mind. Once a child has ventured beyond earthly restrictions, he or she can never crawl back into old mental modes of thought. Let us not be afraid of affording our children the opportunity to use their supple and energetic minds. Our world has such a desperate need for men or women of character, who esteem others, who promote excellence in values and morality. Fairy tales and fantasy help children to find themselves – their best selves.

The great master of literature, Leo Tolstoy, wrote: "To teach and educate a child is impossible and senseless on the simple ground that the child stands nearer than I do to that ideal of harmony, truth, beauty and goodness which I wish to lead him." And yet, Tolstoy continued to write for children, leaving 600 folk and fairy tales for their enlightenment. His profoundly simple tales speak to the most basic questions and he considered these tales to be his most important work.

Fantasy and folktales do relate specifically to the conditions of contemporary society. Ask students if they recognize Hitler or Osama Bin Laden in Watership Down. Surely Hans Christian Andersen's The Nightingale is a powerful comment on what modern technology could be doing to our values as it outraces conservation of nature. It is significant that so many outstanding thinkers tell of a childhood rich with fairy tales and fantasy. When Albert Einstein was asked what children should read that would best help them to become scientists, his response was "fairy tales."

If children are at home in fairy tale and fantasy land, perhaps they can help to make our world a bit more secure. If they have reached a higher resource beyond pure knowledge and reason, if they have caught a vision from a myth, if they have been touched by inspiration in a fantasy, their lives will attest to their faith. Having spoken freely with their most noble ancestors in folk tales, who have shared eternal convictions in the power of love and freedom, tomorrow's children will be able to create a new history.

Kornei Chukovsky, a most beloved author of books for Russian children, has said about childhood, "The young child uses fantasy as a means of learning, and adjusts it to reality in the exact amounts his need demands. The present belongs to the sober, the cautious, the routine-prone, but the future belongs to those who do not rein in their imaginations."

INTRODUCING FAIRY TALE CHARACTERS

Introductory Activities

Topic Talking Give a topic related to what will be studied. Partner A speaks on the topic to Partner B until the teacher says "switch." B speaks to A until the teacher says "stop."
Round One: Topic: fairy tale characters (10 seconds) **Round Two**: Topic: Delivering a message. (20 seconds). **Round Three**: Topic: Holes (30 seconds). **Purpose**: To pull from students' experiences and to develop oral language facility.
Brainstorming How many ways can you think of to deliver a message?

WHOLE CLASS READERS THEATRE

Many children read the same part at the same time in a shared reading experience. Adapted from: A Troll in a Hole by Patricia and Fred McKissack. Milliken, 1989. With permission. Characters: Boy, Troll, Elf, Knight, Giant's Wife, Princess, Narrator

BOY: One sunny day I was taking a stroll when I came upon a deep hole. Sitting at the bottom was a sad little troll. He said:

TROLL: Boy, go to town and toll the bell so the people will come and help me out of this hole.

BOY: I'm sorry, Troll, but I have to get to school. But look, there's an elf. I'll ask her to take the message. Elf, will you go to town and toll the bell so the people will come and help an old troll out of a mole hole?

ELF: I'm going to the shoemaker's now, but I'll take the message as far as I can. There's a knight passing by. I'll give him the message. Please, Sir Knight, will you go to town and toll the bell and tell the people that a troll who collects the toll on the road has found a whole lot of gold in an old mole hole?

KNIGHT: I have to go slay a dragon right now, but I'll stop by the giant's castle and leave the message with Mrs. Giant. Madam, will you go to town and toll the bell and tell the people to hide their gold for there's a moldy old troll waiting to jump from his coal hole and rob the travelers along the road?

MRS. GIANT: I have to fix the giant's dinner, but I'll give the message to the next princess who rides by.

PRINCESS: I was riding by the giant's castle when Mrs. Giant ran out and gave me a frightening message. I told my coachman, "Step on it." I got to town and rang the bell. "Loyal subjects," I shouted, "A band of bold trolls is coming to town! They will take all your young ones and hide them in holes unless every household gives every troll gold.

NARRATOR: The sun was directly overhead when the angry people got ready for a **Big** battle. They went out to find the band of trolls. They looked along the road. Then they found a hole. But sitting at the bottom was only one very small, very sad troll. Just then, the boy who had found the troll came back from his stroll.

BOY: GOOD! I SEE YOU ALL GOT MY MESSAGE!

READING THE WORLD WITH FOLKTALES

1. LET'S GO TO CHINA
THE JOURNEY OF MENG by Doreen Rappaport. Dial 1991.

Meng's scholar husband is sent to work on the building of the Great Wall. The workers are treated badly by the cruel emperor and many die including Meng's husband. She is determined to take his bones back to their home but must seek the emperor's permission.

Activity Learn about the Great Wall of China. In a small group, guess the answers to these questions: How old is the wall? In what part of China is it located? How tall? How wide in feet? How long in miles? Check your answers by reading about the wall in the encyclopedia.

Action Pattern

If I were in charge of _____

There would be _____

You wouldn't have _____ I'd cancel _____

But the most important thing I would do is_____

2. LET'S GO TO SOUTH AFRICA
ABIYOYO by Pete Seeger. Macmillan, 1988.

A boy and his trickster father are banished from the village until they outwit the giant, Abiyoyo.

Activity Before reading, write a paragraph to describe an African giant. Read the tale through once and decide where it can be elaborated upon. What appropriate words, sounds etc. can you add to bring the tale alive?

3. LET'S GO TO PERU

CHANCAY AND THE SECRET OF FIRE by Donald Charles. Putnam's, 1992.

Chancay must face fierce panthers, erupting volcanos and lightning bolts to win the secret of fire for his people. Use the information in the **Llama Data Bank** in the pattern:

Lives	**Eats**	**Has**
Peru	shrubs	thick hair
mountains	grasses	four legs

Does	**Looks Like**
carries loads	five feet tall
spits	brown, buff & gray
travels 20 miles daily	white or black

Use the information in this pattern:

Hey kids, I have a llama for sale. It's the handiest thing you would ever want to own because it can_____

_____and _____

and_____, but the greatest thing about it is _____ .

4. LET'S GO TO CANADA
THE GHOST HORSE OF THE MOUNTIES by Sean O'Huigin. David Godine Pub. 1991.

A young Mountie is killed and his horse disappears during a storm that causes a stampede. Years later the old horse finds the Mountie's grave and dies beside his master.

Activity Choose which you would be – a Mountie or a wild horse. Use this pattern to write about yourself:

If I were a _____

(Tell where)_____

(Doing what?)_____

I would _____

And _____

If I were a _____.

5. LET'S GO TO MEXICO
THE SLEEPING BREAD by Stefan Czernecki and Timothy Rhodes. Hyperion Books, 1992.

Beto, the baker always had bread to give the beggar, Zafiro. To prepare for a big celebration, the townspeople ban all beggars from the town. As Zafiro bids Beto good bye, a tear falls into the water jar used to make the dough. The next morning the bread won't rise. Has the village lost more than a beggar?

Activity Read about Mexico and complete this pattern:

If I visited Mexico

I could _____

And _____

And _____

I would see_____

and _____

But I couldn't see wildlife in Denali National Park because visitors to Alaska do that.

6. LET'S GO TO RUSSIA
SALT by Alexander Afanasiev. from <u>Russian Fairy Tales</u>. Random House. 1976.

A merchant father sends his three sons in cargo-laden ships to make their fortunes. The two older sons lost their cargos but the youngest son, Ivan, finds an island with a mountain of salt and trades the salt to the Tsar for gold, silver, jewels and the Tsar's daughter. On the return journey Ivan sees his brothers' battered ships and takes them aboard. The jealous brothers toss Ivan overboard and make their way home with the Tsar's daughter. With the help of a giant, Ivan arrives home just in time to put things straight and to marry the Tsar's daughter proving that he is not so much of a fool as everyone thought.

ABOUT RUSSIA

Today Russia is an independent nation but many years ago the land was ruled by a Tsar. Most royal families lived in St. Petersburg which is today called Leningrad. The largest city in Russia is Moscow. There are few private homes. Most children go to school for ten years. In the time of the Tsars, Russia was a part of the Soviet Union which was so large that when people in Moscow were going to bed, those in Vladivostock were having breakfast.

Activity Make a True/False Book About Russia. Make a statement about Russia on one page. **Example** "For hundreds of years Russia was called the sleeping bear of the world." Ask your reader if this statement is fact or fiction. On the next page, tell the reader the answer and explain why. **Example** Fact: Long after other countries had modern factories, the people of Russia were farming using the same hand tools their ancestors used to till the land.

Activity Sharing the story in song (Tune: "My Bonnie Lies Over the Ocean")

Young (1) I ___ sailed over the ocean.
Most people thought he was a (2) f_____
But while at sea (3) I_____ would learn more
Than if he were going to (4) s_____ .
Chorus:
Ivan questioned
The shape of the (5) E_____Was it flat or (6) r_____?
(7) F_____ answered
"It's flat, son, just look at the(8) g_____ .

The boy traded(9) s_____for some treasures
His brothers threw him (10) o_____
Then counted the (11) g_____and the (12) s_____
A truly magnificent hoard.

Key: 1.Ivan 2.fool 3.Ivan 4.school 5.Earth 6.round 7.Father 8.ground 9.salt 10.overboard 11.gold 12. silver

The Wolfhound by Kristine Franklin. Lothrop, 1997.
    In Tsarist Russia, for a commoner to own a wolfhound was to risk prison or worse. Paval rescues a wolfhound in a snowstorm and cannot abandon her.
Activity What should Paval do to assure the dog's safety? List your ideas on the decision grid that follows.

Ideas	Fast	Safe for boy	Safe for dog	Low Cost	Will Work	Total

Score: 1=no 2=maybe 3=yes
  Activity Report on Russia in a Geo Poem.
  Name: Russia
  Two features: Frozen land, many languages
  Three activities: Sleighride, folkdance, sightsee
  Four sights: Kremlin, Hermitage, Moscow, Troikas
  Describe: Country of emerging freedom

CINDERELLA TALES FROM AROUND THE WORLD

1. TATTERCOATS Illus by Margot Tomes. Putnam's, 1989.
   Rejected by her grandfather, Tattercoats is given rags to wear and kitchen scraps to eat. Only the gooseherd could cheer her up. When the king announces a ball to find a bride for the prince, the gooseherd proposes that they travel together to see the palace. The trip provides unexpected surprises as the gooseherd's pipes work their magic.

Activity Create a **Fact and Fiction Book** about the British Isles.

Activity **Take a poll** Which sight would classmates most like to see in Great Britain? The changing of the guard? The Royal jewels? The statue of Peter Pan?

2. YEH-SHEN, A CINDERELLA STORY FROM CHINA by Ai-Ling Louie, Philomel, 1982.
   Yeh-Shen's stepmother killed and ate her only friend, a small fish. Yeh-Shen buries the fish bones and wishes on them to receive beautiful clothes to attend the festival. But she loses a slipper and when she returns home the bones are silent. Little does she know that the Emperor is seeking the owner of the slipper.

Activity What would the character do? Answer for both Yeh-Shen and the Stepmother.
   1. If she were all alone in a strange city?
   2. If she found a hungry puppy on the road?
   3. If she were granted one wish?

3. THE ROUGH FACE GIRL by Rafe Martin. Putnam's, 1992.
   Her sisters dressed beautifully but could not answer strange questions put to them by the sister of the Invisible Being, thus, neither cruel sister could become his wife. The Rough-Face Girl, dressed in tree bark and cracked moccasins has better luck!

Activity Describe an Indian Village in a Riddle Poem.
Let's go to long ago places and see the Earth's changing faces. (List 6-8 sights)
But that's not all. List 6-8 more sights.
Where am I?

4. Let's Visit the Appalachian Mountains with **ASHPET, AN APPALACHIAN TALE** by Joanne Compton. Holiday House, 1994.

Activity Before reading this Cinderella variant, answer these questions.
   Where would she live?
   What jobs will she do?
   Who would all the girls want to marry?
   What would be the big event all want to attend?
   Who will help Ashpet?
   What will her new dress be made of?
   What will she lose?

Activity Try creating a Cinderella tale from another time or place. Research the culture of the time and place to answer the above questions. **For example** A California Cinderella would be very different from a Texas Cinderella. A stone age Cinderella would be very different from a Colonial Cinderella.

CREATE A CINDERELLA TALE

SISTERS: Look at our sister! She is so plain that we want nothing to do together with her. All she's good for is work!

GIRL: How can I possibly finish all of these tasks in one day? I must (name five or six tasks) and then prepare the (name ethnic foods) for my mother and sisters to take to the _____.

SISTERS: What is that we hear? A _____ approaching? It must be (name male character).

NARRATOR ONE: The mother and sisters went out to meet the _____. Away they went leaving (heroine's name) in tears with only _____ for company.

GIRL: I shall never finish all these tasks. But wait, what is that sound? I hear _____.

NARRATOR TWO: When the servant girl opened the door she saw (rescuer) _____. (Rescuer) looked at (heroine) _____ and (tell what the rescuer did) Not only was _____ dressed in a beautiful _____ but a _____ was waiting to take her to the _____ . She knew, however, that the magic would only last until _____ and that she must return home by then.

NARRATOR ONE: At the (event), the (male character) asked (girl) to _____ and the time went so quickly that she knew she must leave at once. She tossed her _____ into the _____ pretending that she had lost it and when (male hero) went to look for it, she hurried back to the _____ as quickly as she could.

NARRATOR TWO: Word soon spread that the (male hero) was visiting every _____ seeking the owner of the _____ .

MOTHER: Here he comes! You must both claim to be the owner of the _____ and do your best to make it fit. You may not have another chance! Quickly, hide (heroine) _____ in the _____ .

HERO: There is no use in the two of you trying this _____ on. It is obviously too _____. Yet I have visited every _____ in the _____ _____ and there is no one left to try.

Tell how the hero discovers the poor girl and what happens to the stepmother and stepsisters.

FAIRY TALE WRITING ACTIVITIES

1. **Create a book** titled **A** IS FOR FAIRY TALE (Accounts of amazing action) using the pattern in Q is for Duck by Mary Elting. Clarion, 1980.
_____ is for _____ because _____
S is for **Rumpelstiltskin** because **he saved the miller's daughter by spinning straw into spools of golden thread.**

2. **Share** The Three Bears by James Marshall. Houghton Mifflin, 1991.
Write a defense for Goldilocks as to why she should not be jailed for breaking, entering and vandalizing the Three Bears' property.

3. **Homophones** See books by Fred Gwynne: The King Who Rained, Simon & Schuster, 1970, A Little Pigeon Toad, Simon & Schuster, 1988.
Write a sentence about a fairy tale character that contains two homophones.
Example When Snow White saw the dwarfs, she thought the miners might be minors.

4. Jack and the Beanstalk by Steven Kellogg. Morrow, 1997.
Choose three or four of the items below and **write an excuse** for Jack to tell his mother as to why he took beans for the cow.

old	shoe	crazed rabbit	a key	a troll	old bridge
a map	quicksand	singing toad	2 candles	straw hut	golden egg
a haircut					

5. **Compare** two fairy or folktale characters using this pattern:
If I had the _____ of _____
I would _____ and I would _____
But I wouldn't _____ because _____ does that.

Example
   If I had the feet of Jack
   I'd climb beanstalks and I'd steal the giant's hen and harp
   But I wouldn't lose a glass slipper
   Because Cinderella does that.

6. **A Writing Pattern** Brown Bear, Brown Bear by Bill Martin, Jr. Holt, 1970.
   Rapunzel, Rapunzel what do you see?
   I see a prince looking at me.
   Prince, prince, what do you see?
   I see a witch coming toward me.

7. <u>Heckedy Peg</u> by Audrey and Don Wood. Harcourt, 1987.
Help the mother save her children by **matching** the food on the table with the gift each asked for.

8. Choose one incident that follows and **write three sentences explaining your choice**:
Would you rather:
Spin straw into gold **or** turn anything you touched into gold?
Fall asleep for 100 years **or** be changed into a frog?
Be able to lie **or** be unable to tell the truth?
Have a wolf **or** have a troll for a friend?

9. Create a **fairy tale newspaper**. A lead story might be "Pig Sues Wolf for Damages"
(From <u>The True Story of the Three Little Pigs</u> by John Scieszka. Viking PRess. 1989.)

10. Creative Cause and Effect
Ask questions about a character's actions. Use at least three ideas in the answer.
Example Why did Goldilocks go into the bear's house?
"I like exploring new places. I was lost and seeking help. When I see an open door, I can't help myself. I must enter."

11. Reporting on a Setting Follow this pattern.

Let us go to fairy tale places
And see that world's various faces
We will find:
Fields of poppies
Surrounding a high wall
A gatekeeper guarding the entrance
Towers seen in the distance
But that's not all:
Music floating in the air
Windows sparkling like jewels
Rays of green light touching everything
Where am I?
The Emerald City, of course.

THE WONDERFUL WIZARD OF OZ by L. Frank Baum

1. Topic Talking Partners speak on three topics related to what they will be reading. <u>Round One</u>: A speaks to B five seconds on "A Journey. The leader says "Switch" and B speaks to A for five seconds. Follow with <u>Round Two</u>, ten seconds, and <u>Round Three</u>, fifteen seconds. Topics are: a tornado, a journey, friendship.

2. Topic Focusing Answer by guessing the correct number.

A. A tornado is about _____yards across.

B. Its winds blow at _____ miles per hour.

C. The average tornado sweeps a path ____miles long at a speed of ____ to ___ miles per hour.

D. How much time does it take to complete its destruction in any one place?_____minutes. Read about tornadoes to support or deny guesses.

3. Creative Writing Use metaphors to describe the dusty gray funnel. What does it remind you of? (**Example** an elephant's trunk.) What does it do that a person does? (sweeping up.) How or where does it do it? (the crumbs of the prairie.)

<u>Sentence</u>: The dusty gray funnel is an elephant's trunk sweeping up the crumbs of the prairie. Use the same pattern to describe: the whirling house, the bending grass, or the wailing wind.

4. Vocabulary

prairie	whirlwind	amazement	luscious
sorceress	Munchkins	hesitate	bondage
civilized	journey	curious	danger
earnest	tedious	witch	dismal
reproach	confidential	patient	oblige
enchanted	inconvenient	anxious	astonished
motionless	dangerous	misfortune	awkward
enable	industrious	monstrous	discouraged
aroused	fragrance	reflection	spectacles
clumsy	Scarecrow	cruelty	Dorothy
destroy	weapons	companions	prosperous

Sentence structure: Use all the words in one section in one sentence to describe Dorothy's arrival in Oz.

5. Pre Reading Journal

Choose one sentence starter and write for five minutes. Share orally with a small group.

A. In a civilized country people . . .

B. A lighted match can cause trouble when . . .

C. An unexpected journey would be . . .

6. Dorothy the Immigrant

One who arrives in a new land to live is called an immigrant. A rich mix of people in any nation results in creativity and change.

Choose two famous immigrants and compare them using this pattern:

    If I were (name)

    I would (accomplishment)

    And I'd (more information)

    But I wouldn't (accomplishment of 2nd person)

    Because (name) did that.

7. The Road Through the Forest

Trees protect the forest by picking up intruders in their branches and tossing them back on the road. It takes 75,000 trees to produce one Sunday edition of the New York Times.

Brainstorm: In two minutes, how many ways can you list to save paper?
Forecast what will happen if we lose all of the forests in North America.

If trees protect the forest by picking up intruders in their branches and tossing them back on the road, how can the travelers get past these trees?

Ideas	Fast	Safe	Possible	Will Work	Total

1=no 2=maybe 3=yes

8. The Tin Woodman Wants a Heart

In 1900 when Baum wrote this story, there were no heart transplants. In the future it is predicted:

    _____ A. Replacement organs will be grown from a patient's own cells.

    _____ B. Wires from a TV camera to a blind person's brain will allow the person to see.

    _____ C. Most people will live to age 150.

    _____ D. Artificial ears that work will be common.

Put the above items in order, listing the one you think is most important first.

9. Proverbs (Reading comprehension)

Tell how the proverb is related to one of the characters in The Wonderful Wizard of Oz.

A. Don't cry over spilt milk.

B. Still waters run deep.

C. Let sleeping dogs lie.

D. Actions speak louder than words.

E. Two wrongs don't make a right.

10. Search for the Wicked Witch

The Wicked Witch of the West sends a pack of wolves to attack the travelers.
Fact: 8% of the 500,000,000 species that have existed on earth since the beginning of time are extinct.

Activity Create a data bank about an endangered species: List four places it lives, four things it eats, four things it does and four things it has. Use the information in one of the animal reporting pattern that follows.

Endangered Species Data Bank

Lives

_____

_____

_____

_____

Eats

_____

_____

_____

_____

Has

_____

_____

_____

_____

Does

_____

_____

_____

_____

---

11. The Discovery of Oz, the Terrible
Oz is a humbug who cannot grant the friends' wishes. Use at least four of these items in an excuse the Oz might give as to why he cannot give the Tin Woodman a heart.

an old shoe	a crazed rabbit	vanishing cream
six crows	a giant fish	moaning oak tree
a troll	blackberry pie	a singing toad
a red cape	quicksand	a collapsed bridge

12. Have a Contest!
Which team can name two things found in nature that begin with each letter of **R A I N B O W** ? Do not include animals.

13. Trust, Friendship and Love
In a future global village, perhaps the most important qualities will be trust, friendship and love . . . themes of L.Frank Baum's classic.
Share <u>My Love for You</u> by Susan Roth
 . . . is larger than one bear, taller than two giraffes . . . (add more animals up to ten)

DESCRIPTIVE WRITING EXERCISE

From: THE LITTLE MERMAID by Hans Christian Anderson

When writing to describe you must:

1. Use colorful and specific words.
2. Add details to create good descriptions.
3. Use the five senses. Let your reader see, touch, taste, smell and hear.

In a descriptive essay:

Paragraph One: Tell the reader what the essay is about and why you want the reader to have the information.

Paragraph Two: The body of the essay gives a clear description. The excerpt below would be paragraph two describing the place where the wicked sea witch lives.

Paragraph Three: The conclusion. Summarize your thoughts and tell how you feel about the topic.

Use descriptive words and phrases in the paragraph below.

The Little Mermaid went out of her 1._____ and swam toward the

2._____ whirlpool where the sea witch lived. No 3._____ grew

there, only 4._____ sand stretched toward the pool, where the water

like a 5. _____ whirled around. She traveled a path of 6._____ slime. The

trees on either side reached out with 7._____ arms. Every one of them

had caught something. There were 8._____ and 9._____

clutched tight and skeletons of 10._____. Water snakes wallowed in the mud

showing their 11._____bellies. In the middle of the clearing stood a

house made of 12._____ and there sat the 13._____

sea witch with a 14._____ in her mouth, a 15._____

round her neck and 16._____which covered her hands and feet.

ACTIVITIES WITH THE HARRY POTTER BOOKS

Harry Potter has never been the star of a Quidditch team, scoring points while riding a broom far above the ground. He knows no spells, has never helped to hatch a dragon, and has never worn a cloak of invisibility.

All he knows is a miserable life with the Dursleys, his horrible aunt and uncle, and their abominable son, Dudley, a great big swollen spoiled bully. Harry's room is in a tiny closet at the foot of the stairs, and he hasn't had a birthday party in eleven years.

But all that is about to change when a mysterious letter arrives by owl messenger. The letter is an invitation to an incredible place that Harry will find unforgettable. For it is at Hogwarts School of Witchcraft and Wizardry that Harry finds not only friends, aerial sports, and magic in everything from classes to meals, but a great destiny that's been waiting for him if he can survive the encounter

1. Topic Talking Partner A talks to B on three topics related to the novel increasing the time for each round.

2. Topic Focusing Guess the answers.
  A. Great Britain is how many miles long?_____
  B. Great Britain is how many miles wide?_____
  C. How many ruling Kings has Great Britain had since 1707?____
  D. How many ruling Queens ?_____
  E. Great Britain has ___times as many people as live in Oregon.

Read to support or deny your guesses.

Great Britain is the largest island in Europe and the seventh largest island in the world. While it is nearly the same size in area as Oregon, it has thirty times as many people. The distance from east to west is 320 miles. The distance from north to south is 600 miles. From 1707 when Scotland, England and Wales were joined, Great Britain has had nine ruling kings and three ruling queens.

3. Vocabulary Which team can use the most words in ONE sentence to describe the cover of one of the Potter novels?

Muggles	Medieval	ravenous	parchment
cauldron	separation	detention	instant
souvenir	flinch	nanosecond	bizarre
unconscious	gaunt	abnormal	expulsion
annoyance	wastrel	apoplectic	massacre
warlock	suspicious	apothecary	illuminated
reinforcement	woebegone	sarcastic	embarrassed
disgruntle	infuriating	furtive	levitate
apprehensive			

4. Magic Poetry

Choose one of the magic items Harry learned to use at the school. You might choose a broomstick, a magic wand, a cauldron, a cloak of invisibility, or a mirror that tells the future. Write about the item using the pattern that follows.

_____(Name the item.)

They call me _____

The colors that surround me are_____

And remind one of _____

As an employee at Hogwarts I _____

My garments are _____ and _____

My energy source is _____

I am related to _____

I vacation at _____

And without my services Hogwarts' students would_____

5. A Game of Words

The author creates many unusual situations in this novel from riding on firebolts, which are high performance broomsticks, to meeting Parslemouths, wizards who can talk to snakes. In order to create new characters, places and objects, the author must also create new words. You, too, can be creative by playing with words in a different way. Look at the words that follow. Choose two and combine them to make a new compound word. Then tell how a wizard would use this new thing. Create an illustrated dictionary of at least ten words.

break	wind	broad	work	home	water
tooth	light	flash	leader	cheer	time
supper	board	card	sty	pig	sauce
apple	worm	meal			

Example Combine foot and pick to make the new word footpick.
When a wizard wants to dig up his gold he says magic words to turn his foot into a pick and starts digging.

6. Brainstorm

A. Reasons to love homework.
B. Uses for a shrinking lotion.
C. Uses for a book that walks, snaps and tries to bite when you open it.
D. Uses for an invisible cloak.

7. Analogies

Example Headmaster is to Hogwarts as Postmaster is to Post Office.
Complete these analogies. Add more analogies based on **your** school.

A. Chalk is to chalkboard as pencil is to _____

B. Plants are to nursery as potions are to _____

C. Ghost is to Halloween as _____ is to _____

D. Voldemorts is to evil as Harry is to _____

8. Flexible Thinking Re-write the following sentences, keeping the meaning but eliminating the letter "A."

A. The rain blew hard on the castle walls.

B. The creature cackled and zoomed backwards.

C. Harry waved the magic wand.

9. Rank Order

The author, J. K. Rowling, uses her imagination to create unusual characters and objects. Pepperup Lotion is a cure for colds. Kwickspell is a correspondence course in beginning magic. A Howler is a letter that screams at the recipient. Rank order first to last choice, the following items your group would most to least like to have.

_____ A) Invisibility cloak

_____ B) Shrinking potion

_____ C) A Pocket Sneakoscope

_____ D) A Talking Mirror

_____ E) A Howler Letter

10. Quotes to Think About What do these mean?

"The truth. It is a beautiful and terrible thing, and should therefore be treated with great caution."

"It takes a great deal of bravery to stand up to our enemies, but just as much to stand up to our friends."

"It is our choices, Harry, that show what we truly are, far more than our abilities."

Using pictures from old magazines, illustrate one of the quotes with a collage.

11. Compare Harry Potter to Luke Skywalker in "Star Wars." How many ways can you list that the two characters and the two stories are alike.

Example Both heroes are orphans. Both are guided by an older, wiser person. Both must fight an evil force. Add as many more as you can.

12. <u>Character Analysis</u> What would a character do?

1. Cut apart all of the cards. Place in two stacks on a table.
2. A player picks a card from the character pile and from the incident pile and tells what the character would most likely do if caught in that situation.

1. Harry	2. Hermione	3. Ron	4. Serius Black

5. Professor Snape	6. Professor Lupin	7. Dumbledore	8. Hagrid

A. Your character is alone at night on a dark, deserted street and hears footsteps approaching..	B. Your character is at the supermarket and knocks over a barrel of apples, spilling them all over the floor.	C. Your character answers the door to find a homeless person asking for food.	D. Your character is given the choice of attending a symphony concert or a rock festival.

E. Your character has done a difficult job for agreed-upon pay and the employer refuses to pay.	F. Your character is alone in a strange land where no one speaks the character's language and wants directions for getting home.	G. Your character is on horseback out west and faces a herd of stampeding cattle.	H. Your character was left home alone by mistake. The family won't return for three days.

WHAT KIND OF THINKING ARE WE ASKING STUDENTS TO DO?

PRODUCTIVE THINKING	PROBLEM SOLVING	CRITICAL THINKING	
The student expresses many ideas though not all of the highest quality (Fluency)	The student gives many alternatives to a problem solution	The student can determine the causes and effects of a given situation (Forecasting)	The student is able to look at the parts of a whole and the relationships among parts. (Analyze)
The student can group items in a variety of ways.(Flexibility)	The student is able to weigh alternative using selected criteria.	The student is able to define the basic attributes of a person, place or thing. (Attribute Listing)	The student is able to find common elements among seemingly dissimilar items. (Analogy)
The student expresses unusual or uncommon responses, though not all ideas prove to be of use. (Originality)	The student is able to make a final judgment in terms of alternatives		
The student builds onto a basic idea or product by adding details to make it more interesting or complete. (Elaboration)	The student is able to defend his/her decision by giving many reasons for the choice.		The student is able to examine data, draw a generalization and support or deny generalizations with evidence. (Generalize)

Put the number of each assignment below in the Strategy Box above which shows the type of thinking required.

1. Give six unusual ways for traveling from the Dursleys to Hogwarts.
2. Prepare a chart on European folktales showing character, setting, plot & theme of each. Examine the completed chart. What general statements can you make about European folktales?
3. List all the words you can to describe Norton, the Dragon.
4. Create a data bank about unicorns.
5. Discuss the many ways that the characters of Harry Potter and Peter Pan are alike.
6. Use evidence from the story to predict what will happen next.
7. How many ways can you group the characters from the Harry Potter books?
8. How can Harry save Hermione from the troll? Give several ideas.
9. Give reasons for or against using the Dementors to guard Hogwarts.
10. What could you add to the grounds of Hogwarts School to prevent Voldemort from entering?
11. Apply numerical values to listed ideas in #8 to determine Harry's best course of action in saving Hermione from the troll.
12. Create character comparisons using this pattern: Harry Potter is to nice as Draco Malfoy is to mean.
13. What would be the best way for Harry to save Hermione from the troll ?

Key: Productive: 1.3,7,1,10   Problem Solving: 8,11,13,9,6,4   Critical Thinking: 5,12,2

THE BFG by Roald Dahl. Farrar, 1982.

Pre Reading Activity

The BFG often gets words mixed up and says words like those listed below. Guess the meaning of each word. Put the letter **P** on the line if you think it is a person; **F** if it is a food and **A** if you think it is an animal. Then read the booktalk to support or deny your guesses.

1.	_____	cannybull	6.	_____	strawbunkles
2.	_____	hippodumpling	7.	_____	childers
3.	_____	crocadowndilly	8.	_____	tottlers
4.	_____	snozcumber	9.	_____	frobscottle
5.	_____	human bean	10.	_____	scrumplet

Sophie trembled in fright. Inside the cave it was as dark as night. The giant who had snatched her from her bed gently lowered her to the floor. Suddenly a blaze of light lit up the cavern.

"Please don't eat me," Sophie begged.

"I am not a cannybull," the giant shouted, "or a hippodumpling or crocadowndilly like you have in your zoo. They eat anything. I only eat snozcumbers."

"Why did you steal me out of my bed?" Sophie asked.

"Because, you poor little scrumplet, you saw me out of your window. You would have told everyone that giants exist. We simply can't have that so you will just have to stay with me for the rest of your life. Don't worry, I'll protect you from the bad giants."

"What bad giants?" Sophie asked.

"The ones that eat little tottlers," said the BFG. "Human beans and especially little childers is like strawbunkles and cream to those giants. Here, have a nice drink of frobscottle."

The more Sophie learns about the other horrible giants who guzzle little childers all over the world, the more she is determined to stop their guzzling. With the help of the BFG who collects dreams in bottles, the Queen of England and the Royal Air Force, Sophie cooks up and carries out her plan. To find out how it all happens, read The BFG!

Step One	Step Two	Step Three
Choose and circle one action word	Choose and circle one topic	Choose and circle one product
Label	**Research Projects**	Acrostic poem
List	*Life in a real castle.	Chart
Describe	*Three differences in living in England today and living in the United States.	Model
Locate		Mystery Report
Report	*Famous sights you would see in the city of London today.	10 Reasons Report
Show		Bio-poem
Compare	*Famous person from Great Britain.	Fortunately Report
Discover		True/false book
Compose		
Create		

Sample Statement: I will describe the life and work of a famous person from Great Britain in a Fortunately Report.

The Fortunately Report

Fortunately Roald Dahl's books are loved by children.
Unfortunately his teachers called him illiterate, lazy and a muddler with limited ideas.
Fortunately he got through school successfully.
Unfortunately he did not begin to write until age 26.
Fortunately he was able to travel the world in his job.
Unfortunately World War II was declared.
Fortunately he survived World War II as a fighter pilot for the British Air Force.
Unfortunately his youngest child was badly injured in an accident.
Fortunately with Dahl's help, the child survived.
Unfortunately his wife, the actress Patricia Neal, became very ill.
Fortunately he nagged her into recovery so that she could act again.
Unfortunately some of Dahl's books for children are now out of print.
Fortunately many have been made into movies.

EXPANDING HORIZONS WITH NOVELS

All children should have the opportunity to wonder. Children are so easily catapulted into the world of pure academia, a world of fact and figures and reason. But without the wonder, the humanness of compassion, charity and empathy, where is the link to bind all people together? We must keep on the alert not to bypass those sharp perceivers who will help the world to find answers to living together in harmony. Enlightened authors of junior novels with lucid minds and fresh styles for communicating ideas can help. It is the authors who do not blunt their pens when they write for children, who lift us all to a clearer view of ourselves and our reason for being, whose words ignite us. We are blessed by many dedicated and gifted writers who have the ability to stretch young minds into previously unexplored worlds. Jean Merrill, Avi, Joan Aiken, Louis Sachar and Ted Hughes are among many.

Books such as Jean Merrill's <u>Pushcart War</u> can reinforce an awareness of the indomitable human spirit. Hope, loyalty and courage surmount the many obstacles which must be overcome in Avi's <u>Beyond the Western Sea</u>. <u>The Iron Giant</u> by Ted Hughes leaves one pondering just how far an imagination can stretch. Louis Sachar's <u>Holes</u> can impel a reader to contemplate the meaning of responsibility, to recognize courage and resourcefulness.

Our children do not need more and more words bombarding them from all sides. They need deeper, more beautiful, more heart-stretching and mind-stretching ideas to confront. They need to be offered books with a variety of levels of meaning to free their minds for the gymnastics of which they are capable. Caring parents and teachers are the guides on these literary journeys, first to introduce to the literature and then to listen and value children's responses to it.

HISTORICAL FICTION

BEYOND THE WESTERN SEA - BOOK ONE - ESCAPE FROM HOME by AVI.
Orchard Books, 1996.

About The Book

It is 1851. Maura and Patrick O'Connell, fifteen and twelve-year-old Irish peasants, seek to escape a country destroyed by famine and the greed of English landlords. For Sir Laurence Kirkle, eleven and son of one such English lord, America holds the promise of justice, though he steals a fortune from his father to get there. How the O'Connells and young Laurence come to share a common fate in the English city of Liverpool, embarkation port for America, makes for an adventure alive with ironic coincidence and surprise.

1. Topic Focusing

Answer the following questions. Guess if you do not know. Support or deny your guesses by reading the paragraph.

A. Between 1840 and 1960, how many immigrants came to the United States (Answer in millions) _____

B. Of the total number of immigrants in (A) how many were Irish? _____

C. In 1860, how many out of every 100 people in the United States came from other lands? _____

D. In the 1840s and 50s what percent of Irish citizens lived on small farms and fed their families mainly potatoes? _____

E. When the potato crop was destroyed by disease in 1845 and 1847, how many Irish died of starvation? _____

F. During this same time, how many Irish emigrated to the United States? _____

In the 1840s and 50s, over half of all Irish citizens worked on small farms or for wealthy British landowners. Their main food was the potato and over one million died of starvation when the crop failed in 1845 and 1847. Another million came to the United States where 13 out of every 100 people were from other lands. The total of immigrants who came to the United States between 1840 and 1860 was 4,311,465.

2. Introducing Vocabulary

Write these words on separate slips of paper. Arrange as many of the words as you can in one sentence to describe one or more of the pictures on the front cover. You may add other words as needed with the exception of conjunctions.

devastated	woe	famine	misfortune
proclaim	cowering	hostile	prosperous
mockery	constable	remorse	agitated
congenial	insurrection	indignation	blighted
trepidation	scrutinize	distinguished	composure
scoundrel	alcove	pandemonium	deceitful

3. Pre Reading Journal Sentence Starters
Choose one for each section of the novel (before reading that section). Complete the sentence and write about the topic for five minutes. Be prepared to share orally what you have written with a small group.

SECTION ONE: Pages 1-99
A. An unexpected knock at a door by a man dressed in black can lead to . . .
B. Watching helplessly while your home is destroyed . . .
C. An unjust punishment can lead to . . .
D. A child alone in a strange city with no money . . .
E. Putting yourself in the hands of strangers . . .

SECTION TWO: Pages 100-203
A. A lodging house in the worst part of a city . . .
B. Discovering that you are a prisoner of one you thought was a friend . . .
C. Having an ulterior motive means . . .
D. Ways to get money when you have none . . .
E. Those who avoid the police are . . .

SECTION THREE: Pages 203-295
A. When no one believes the truth . . .
B. A guilty conscience can lead to actions that . . .
C. The fate of a stowaway if caught is . . .
D. Those who have money can always . . .
E. Putting yourself in danger to help another . . .

4. Chapter Activities
Chapters One to Seven: Summary
The O'Connells receive a letter from their father sending money for their passage to America. At the same time, their home is burned to the ground. They set off for Cork and the ship which will be the first part of their journey.
....

Read aloud pages 25-26. Have a debate by dividing the class into two sections. Should they make the trip or should they not make the trip? Then read pages 27-29 to see what happens.

Chapters Eight Through Twenty-Three: Summary
Eleven-year-old Sir Laurence Kirkle is beaten severely by his brother, Albert, with their father's permission. Laurence runs away, taking 1000 pounds from his father's desk. He loses the money to a ruffian on the street. Meanwhile, Lord Kirkle hires Mr. Pickler to find his son and Albert hires Mr. Clemspool to make sure Laurence is not found. Clemspool finds Laurence on the train to Liverpool and pretends to be his friend.
A. Describe the London of the 1850s as Laurence saw it using this model:

London is (color)_____

It sounds like   _____

It smells like   _____

It tastes like   _____

It looks like   _____

It made Laurence feel like _____

B. Find a famous painting. In one paragraph tell which of the characters you have met so far would like the painting. Give reasons why.

Chapters Twenty-Four through Thirty-Four: Summary

After a difficult crossing, Maura and Patrick reach Liverpool. Toggs, an unscrupulous runner, tells them the place they were to stay has burned down. He takes them to a run down lodging house filled with the poorest of the poor. A poor actor, Mr. Drabble, warns them that they might never be able to leave. Meanwhile, Laurence is taken to a hotel by Clemspool and after discovering that he is really the man's prisoner, escapes and is alone on the Liverpool streets with no money.

A. Write a riddle report about one of the story settings: The Village of Killony, London, Liverpool or On board The Queen of the West. Use this model:

Let's go to long ago places and see the Earth's changing faces.

We will see (list 4-6 sights)

But that's not all (list 4-6 more sights)

Do you know where we are?

Give the answer.

B. During this period of time, Victoria was Queen of England. Research her life and report in an acrostic poem or play the "To Test the Truth" game.

THE "TO TEST THE TRUTH" SHOW

Hostess: Welcome to the To Test The Truth Show. Three people are pretending to be Queen Victoria of England but only one is the real queen. It is up to you to decide which one. Now let's meet our guests.

Victoria I: My name is Queen Victoria. I became Queen at the age of eighteen and ruled for 63 years gaining the respect and veneration of my people.

Victoria I:. I was a very young Queen at a time when people did not respect the throne. But during my rule labor conditions improved and education became compulsory.

Victoria III: Being an only child I was carefully reared and had little contact with the outside world so becoming Queen at a young age was quite bewildering for me.

Hostess: Tell us more.

Victoria I: During the fifty years of my reign there were many wars but my leadership brought each to a successful conclusion.

Victoria II: During my reign upper and lower Canada were united and given self-government.

Victoria III: Ignoring my brother's advice, in 1877 I became Empress of India and seized control of Egypt.

Hostess: Now it is time to vote on the real Queen Victoria. We will vote by a show of hands. Is it number 1, number 2, or number 3? Now for the moment you have all been waiting for. Will the real Queen Victoria please stand?

(The real Queen Victoria is #2. Numbers one and three contradict themselves.)

Chapters Thirty-Five Through Fifty-Four: Summary

Patrick disappears and Maura goes looking for him. Laurence meets up with Toggs who enlists his aid in robbing a ship. The police arrive and Toggs runs away. Laurence and Patrick meet on the docks and are taken in by a minister who feeds them. Patrick promises Laurence a ticket to America and finds his way back to Maura. Meanwhile, the police, Mr. Pickle and Mr. Clemspool are all looking for Laurence.

A. Choose one and complete the sentence below:
     spinning wheel, rusty spigot, empty bow, locked safe, tornado, door hinge

     Injustice is like _____ because _____.

B. By now you can see that the life of an immigrant was very hard. Compile a book titled <u>H IS FOR IMMIGRANT</u>. Each page should explain how the **H** word is related to immigrants and be illustrated.

     haggard, hand-to-hand, health officer, hunger, harvest, hoax, harbor, hostility, hardship, homeless, hovel.

Add other **H** words you can think of.

Chapters Fifty-Five Through Seventy-Four: Summary

Another runner, Fred, befriends Laurence and hides him away until it is time to board the ship. Fred hides Laurence in a crate which is put aboard the ship. He tells Patrick that when the ship is underway, Patrick must release Laurence. Patrick, Maura and Mr. Drabble board the ship for America where they learn that anyone who helps a stowaway will receive the same punishment as the stowaway. Patrick knows that if he doesn't help Laurence, Laurence will die.

5. <u>Research Idea</u>

Choose one of these famous immigrants. Compile a data bank about the person. Use the information from the data bank in a report following the sentence directions below.

John Aubudon	Albert Einstein	Enrico Fermi	John Muir
Andrew Carnegie	Irving Berlin	Arturo Toscanini	Greta Garbo
Joseph Pulitzer	Knute Rockne	Alexander Graham Bell	

BIOGRAPHY DATA BANK

Lived (when/where)	Description	Had
_____	_____	_____
_____	_____	_____
_____	_____	_____
		_____
Remembered For	**Related To**	_____
_____	_____	_____
_____	_____	
_____	_____	
_____	_____	

Write an eight sentence biography report that:

1. Has a beginning question that involves the reader.
2. Tells who, what, when, where.
3. Includes action words that tell what is happening.
4. Shows cause and effect.
5. Shows difficulties that were overcome.
6. Tells what others say about the person.
7. Tells of the person's accomplishments.
8. Has a concluding sentence that uses a universal word (we, all of us, everyone, everywhere, everybody, always, nobody, every time, every day)

HISTORICAL FICTION

THE CAY by Theodore Taylor. Doubleday, 1969.

Timothy WAS different. He was huge, and he was very old, and to Philip he seemed ugly. He ate raw fish and believed in JUMBIS. And he was the most stubborn man Philip had ever known.

But after the Germans torpedoed the freighter on which he and his mother were traveling from war-time Curacao to the U. S., Philip found himself dependent on the old West Indian. There were just the two of them cast up on the barren little Caribbean island — three if you counted Stew Cat — and a crack on the head had left Philip blind. The story of their struggle for survival, and of Philip's efforts to adjust to his blindness and to understand the dignified, wise, and loving old man who was his companion, makes memorable reading.

1. Vocabulary

Use as many words as possible in ONE sentence to describe the cover of the book.

Philip	freighter	Timothy	sextant	papaya	outrageous
cay	mussels	submarines	refinery	mumble	mussels
channel	malaria	palm	fronds	conquer	mutiny
alabaster	U-boats	blackouts	hurricane	ballast	noble
sea urchins	explosion	disheartened	koenoekoe		

2. Pre Reading Journal Sentence Starters for The Cay

Chapter One:
  1. Living in a place without seasons . . .
  2. When submarines attack . . .

Chapter Two:
  3. An island that depends upon ships for food and water . . .
  4. Watching a large ship explode is like . . .

Chapter Three:
  5. Drifting for days on the sea in an open raft . . .
  6. Basic survival needs at sea are . . .

3. Chapter Activities

  Chapters One and Two: Summary

  Philip lives in the Dutch West Indies where ships carrying oil from the Island of Curacao are attacked by U-Boats. The year is 1942. Philip's father arranges passage for the boy and his mother on a ship to the states.

  Activity Research German U-Boat activity in the Caribbean in World War II. Create a chart of U-Boat statistics.

  Chapters Three through Six: Summary

  The raft is surrounded by sharks. Philip falls overboard and is rescued by Timothy.

Activity Complete an Ocean Creature Data Bank.

Lives	**Eats**	**Has**
warm seas	sea animals	rounded body
West Indies	bony fish	21 ft. length
shallow water	turtles	pointed snout
near shore	seals	sharp teeth
Australia	tuna	warm body

Does	**Other Facts**
swims rapidly	Dangerous to humans
opens jaws wide	Top of ocean food chain
bites prey	Bites but rarely eats humans
waits for blood loss	
before eating	

Use the Data Bank information in a **Mystery Report**.
List ten facts (clues)
Ask a classmate to give a number between 1-10.
Read the clue for that number.
The student can guess or pass.
The game continues until the mystery creature is guessed or all clues are read.

Chapters Seven Through Nine: Summary

Philip and Timothy arrive on a small island surrounded by high coral reefs. Timothy goes to explore and Philip becomes frightened to be left alone. Philip rebels when told he has to work and lashes out verbally at Timothy who hits him.

Activity Island Analogies: How many can you write?

Example Coral is to island as claws are to bear. (Both protect themselves by ripping and tearing.) What can you do with sharks, palm trees, coconuts, grass hut, wild birds, fish, hurricane, palm fronds, tide pool?

Chapters Ten and Eleven: Summary

Timothy is convinced that Stew Cat is an evil spirit who prevents help from arriving.

Activity Complete these superstitions in a new way. Be as original as you can.

1. Breaking a mirror is _____

2. If you spill salt you should _____

3. Walking under a ladder is _____

4. Bubbles in coffee mean _____

5. A black cat crossing your path _____

Chapters Twelve and Thirteen: Summary

Timothy has a severe attack of malaria. His fever sends him running into the water. Philip pulls him out. Philip feels helpless to do anything about Timothy's illness. The boy learns to catch fish and volunteers to climb the trees for coconuts.

Activity Island Mystery Report

List ten clues or facts about one type of wildlife on the cay. One must be a "give-away" clue. A student gives a number 1-10. Read the clue for that number. The student can guess or pass. The game continues until the answer is guessed or all clues are read.

Chapters Fourteen and Fifteen: Summary

A hurricane hits the island. Philip and Timothy lash themselves to a palm tree. Timothy dies protecting Philip with his body. The storm passes leaving Philip so sad that he is "beyond tears."

Activity Poetic Description

1. Choose one: The rain, The surf, The wind, The island
   Example The rain
2. Place one or two descriptive words before the noun.
   Example The pounding rain
3. Tell what the (rain, wind or surf) reminds you of.
   Example The pounding rain was a battering ram
4. Tell what it does that a person does.
   Example The pounding rain was a battering ram smashing its fist
5. Tell how or where it does the action.
   Example The pounding rain was a battering ram smashing its fist against the angry sea.

Chapters Sixteen Through Nineteen: Summary

Alone Philip buries Timothy and tries to rebuild his island home. He is attacked by wild birds and by a moray eel as he tries to fish. He hears planes overhead and sets the signal fire. A rescue party arrives and Philip is reunited with his parents.

Activity Use this pattern to write about the ways in which Philip changed from the beginning to the end of the novel.

You are changing, changing.

You feel:	describe the atmosphere _____	
You are:	two adjectives _____	_____
You:	two verbs or verb phrases _____	_____
You are:	color _____	
the color of:	name an object the same color _____	
You are:	give size and shape _____	
and are:	use participle and prepositional phrase _____	

You look at the world with different eyes

as you:	three verb phrases _____	_____
It is:	adjective to move like this _____	
so:	one adjective and one simile _____	
You are:	name _____	

REALISTIC FICTION

HOLES by Louis Sachar. Farrar, Straus & Giroux, 1998.

Stanley Yelnat's family has a history of bad luck, so he isn't too surprised when a miscarriage of justice sends him to a boy's juvenile detention center, Camp Green Lake. There is no lake, it has been dry for over a hundred years, and it's hardly a camp: as punishment, the boys must each dig a hole a day, five feet deep, five feet across, in the hard earth of the dried-up lake bed. The warden claims that this pointless behavior builds character, but that's a lie. Stanley must try to dig up the truth. Because the camp is far from a water source, running away is pointless. No young escapee could reach civilization before dying of thirst. But Zero, Stanley's friend, makes the attempt and just barely survives before being rescued by Stanley, by eating wild onions. When the boys return to camp and decide to dig up a treasure Stanley has found, they are caught in the beam of the warden's flashlight and find themselves standing in a lizard nest. The bite of a yellow-spotted lizard is always fatal and Stanley feels one crawling up his neck.

A parallel story of a young frontier school marm turned outlaw turns out to have quite an effect on Stanley's life and future. Is it her treasure, buried long ago, that the warden seeks?

1. Pre Reading Vocabulary

Work with a partner. Cut apart the word cards. Group in as many ways as you can. Give the reason for each grouping. OR Use as many of the words as you can in a sentence to (1) describe the cover of the book or (2) tell what you think the book will be about. Add other words as needed.

juvenile	grimace	detention	backwards	enraged
embarrassed	depressing	punishment	outlaw	sneakers
lizard	auctioned	obstacles	rampage	ominously
assignments	warden	deputy	Greenlake	indescribable
torturous	surrender	proficient	innovative	ferocious
inexcusable	exasperated	incarcerate	underestimate	ultimatum

2. Introducing Characters with Readers Theater

Narrator:

There is no lake at Camp Greenlake. It is just a dry, flat wasteland. There used to be a town of Greenlake but the town shriveled up and died along with the lake and the people who lived there. A hammock stretches between the only two trees. It belongs to the warden. The warden owns the shade. Out on the lake rattlesnakes and scorpions find shade under rocks and in the holes dug by the campers. Being bitten by a scorpion or a rattlesnake is not the worst thing that can happen to you. You won't die. But you don't want to be bitten by a yellow-spotted lizard. That's the worst thing that can happen to you. You will die a slow and painful death. Always. There's nothing anyone can do to you any more.

Stanley:

My name is Stanley Yelnats. Yelnats is Stanley spelled backwards. The judge gave me a choice, go to jail or go to Camp Green Lake. Being a poor kid I'd never been to a camp before. I'm fat, I have no friends and I always seem to be in the wrong place at the wrong time. I try to be hopeful about life even when my hopes are crushed more times than not. My hero in the NBA is Sweetfeet Livingston and it's his sneakers the judge said I stole. I swear I didn't. They just fell out of the sky. But it doesn't matter. Here I am and it won't be long before these tough kids make buzzard meat out of me. My dad says the reason the Yelnats have such bad luck is because of my no-good-dirty-rotten-pig-stealing-great-great-grandfather who had a curse put on him and all his heirs by a gypsy.

Zero:

Three guesses why they call me Zero. Your first one's right. There's nothing inside my head. I don't talk much. Ain't got nothin' to say. I'm so dumb I didn't know that old beat up pair of sneakers I stole belonged to a famous basketball player and were going to be auctioned off for 5000 dollars. Soon as I found out I threw them away off the top of an overpass. That ain't what I'm here for though. Judge says there's no hope for me. I'll always be in one jail or another. If I knew how to do two things maybe I could get out of here and not come back. But I can't tell anyone my secret.. I'm too ashamed to admit that I can't read or write.

3. Pre Reading Journal Sentence Starters

Here are open-ended sentence starters to write about before reading this novel. Choose one of the sentence starters to complete and to write about for ten minutes. Write from your own experience on the topic. Be prepared to share your writing orally with a small group.

1. When a person is unjustly accused of a crime . . .

2. A whole town might turn on a person if . . .

3. An inability to read and write can lead to . . .

4. The purpose of a juvenile detention camp is . . .

5. Believing that bad luck is your fate . . .

6. Ways to avoid contact with poisonous desert animals . . .

7. Reasons a person might have no friends are . . .

8. When a person enjoys being cruel to others . . .

9. Standing in a nest of poisonous lizards would call for . . .

10. Being lost in a desert is dangerous because . . .

11. True friendship can be displayed when . . .

12. Superstitious people might believe in a gypsy curse if . . .

4. The Story Setting

Camp Greenlake is located in desert land in a remote part of Texas. The boys at the camp are warned about contact with rattlesnakes and yellow-spotted lizards. Both the boys and animals in the desert must survive in a hostile environment. Intense heat, searing sun and a lack of water are just a few of the challenges to be faced.

Some animals adapt by spending most of the day underground. Rattlesnakes, kangaroo rats and kit foxes are called nocturnal because they only come out at night to eat and hunt. Some animals rarely spend any time above ground. Spadefoot toads spend nine months of every year underground!

Read about animals found in the dry desert area of western Texas. Choose one of the animals and prepare a mystery animal report. List ten clues about the animal. One must be a give-away clue. Ask a classmate to give a number between one and ten. Read the clue for that number. The student can guess or pass. If the guess is not correct or if the student passes, call on another student to give a number. The game continues until the animal is guessed or all clues are read.

Example MYSTERY ANIMAL REPORT

1. I have a naked head.
2. I often vomit when disturbed.
3. I am not known to carry disease.
4. I have an excellent sense of smell.
5. I live with others of my kind.
5. I am found in the southern United States, Texas and desert regions.
6. It is difficult for me to seize and carry food.
7. I live in temperate and tropical regions of America.
8. I am useful because I eat dead bodies that might otherwise decay.
9. I have a graceful, easy soaring flight.
10. I can see great distances. (Answer: vulture)

5. More About the Story Setting

Camp Greenlake is juvenile detention camp for boys who have committed a crime. Each boy spends his day in the hot sun digging a five by five foot hole in the hard desert earth. The smallest infraction of the rule leads to severe punishment by the warden.

Boys and Girls Town is a famous organization that cares for troubled children. Founded in 1917 by Father Edward Flanagan this home has a long history of offering help and hope to children in trouble. Boys Town, as it was then known, became a well-known name with the 1938 MGM movie, "Boys Town" starring Mickey Rooney and Spencer Tracy. Now Boys and Girls town has grown and is located in numerous parts of the United States.

Activity Read about this help for troubled youths on the internet at
http://www.ffbh.boystown.org

Activity
Complete this pattern comparing Camp Greenlake and Boys and Girls Town.

If I lived in Boys and Girls Town,

I might spend my days tending the famous rose garden begun

by_____

Or taking care of _____

I could be driving the tractor in the green fields that supply _____

Or talking with a_____who helps me to find a future

There are plenty of_____

And help if _____

And time for _____ just like all kids my age

And time to think about _____

But I wouldn't be digging five by five foot holes

Or _____

Because boys at Camp Green Lake do that.

6. Questions for Discussion

1. Suppose Stanley had not rescued Zero. How would the story change?

2. How is this story like another story you have read or a television show you have watched?

3. List all the words you can to describe Stanley. Which word best describes him? Why?

4. Why is the setting a main character in the story?

7. Write a Character Cinquain

A great deal can be said in a handful of words, but the words must be chosen with care and they must fit together in some form. This can be achieved by the cinquain, a short five-line poem of eleven words. Under each heading list words that describe Stanley, Zero or Xray.

Appearance	Personality (using "ing" words)	What He Does	His Feelings

Use your words to write a cinquain about the person you chose.
   The form of the cinquain is:
   Line 1: one word for the title
   Line 2: two words describing the title
   Line 3: three words that show action about the title
   Line 4: four words (a phrase) that show feeling
   Line 5: one word (a synonym) for the title

8. About Onions

Onions play a very important role in the story. Here are facts about onions.
   1. One onion contains about 60 calories.
   2. Onions are high in vitamin C.
   3. Onions are a good source of fiber.
   4. Onions have no fat calories.
   5. Onions supply 4% of calcium and 2% of daily iron needs.
   6. Onions contain no cholesterol.

Research additional information and compose an **Ode to An Onion** using this pattern.

   1. I am_____

   2. I dress in_____

   3. I need _____

   4. I am related to_____

   5. I vacation_____

   6. My job is_____

   7. I desire_____

SCIENCE FICTION

THE IRON GIANT: A Story In Five Nights by Ted Hughes. Faber & Faber, Ltd. 1985.

A mysterious creature stalks the land, eating barbed wire and devouring tractors and plows. The farmers are mystified and afraid. Then they glimpse him in the night: the Iron Giant, taller than a house, with glowing headlight eyes and an insatiable taste for metal. The hungry giant must be stopped at all costs.

Only a young boy named Hogarth is brave enough to lead the Iron Giant to a safe home. And only Hogarth knows where to turn when the earth needs a hero . . . a giant hero . . . like never before.

1. A Pre Reading Activity

See what members of your class have in common with the characters and plot of The Iron Giant. Find a different name for each line.

FIND SOMEONE WHO . . .

1. Has visited or lived on a farm. _____
2. Has walked along an ocean beach. _____
3. Who knows what a torso is. _____
4. Has caught fish in a stream. _____
5. Has ridden on a tractor. _____
6. Has seen a real fox. _____
7. Has played a trick on someone. _____
8. Has gone on a picnic. _____

2. Playing with Vocabulary

Using the vocabulary words listed below, make at least five sentences to describe the cover of this book. Try to use at least three of the words in each sentence and add other words as needed. Make your sentences interesting and use your best spelling and punctuation!

iron	nobody	darkness	dustbin
enormous	scattered	seagulls	dangling
immense	breakers	Hogarth	giant
harrows	collapsed	footprints	stupendous
gears	mound	vanished	earthquake
astronomer	Orion	meteorite	wriggling
silhouette	horror	Australia	rumbling
continent	attack	dismay	weapons
strength	champion	telescope	monster
antics	challenge	fierce	astonishment

3. Pre Reading Journal Sentence Starters
Before reading each section of <u>The Iron Giant</u>, choose one of the sentence starters for that section, complete it and continue to write for ten minutes. You will then join a small group to share what you have written.

Chapter One:
1. A story that begins on a high cliff overlooking a deserted beach might be about . . .
2. From a distance, a pile of scrap metal might be mistaken for . . .
3. A small community sometimes does not welcome strangers because . . .

Chapter Two:
1. When children report fantastic things they have seen . . .
2. Capturing a dangerous person can be . . .
3. People who at first appear frightening can often . . .

Chapter Three:
1. A voracious appetite can lead to . . .
2. Peaceful solutions are best when . . .
3. Happiness for a robot would be . . .

Chapter Four:
1. Humans regard creatures from space as . . .
2. If a person's every demand is instantly satisfied, that person will . . .
3. An example of an even contest is . . .

Chapter Five:
1. A slave is . . .
2. Traveling to the sun would not be a good idea because . . .
3. Music can be healing when . . .
4. Peace on Earth is hard to achieve because . . .

4. Questions to Think About
1. Was it right for Hogarth to trick the giant by luring him into the pit? Why or why not?

2. How many ways might the farmers have prevented the giant from eating their machinery other than digging the pit?

3. Why do you suppose the author included the word "angel" in his description of the terrible bat creature?

4. What do you think the author is saying about ways to achieve world peace?

5. How is this story like the story of David and Goliath?

5. Chapter Activities

Chapter One: The Coming of the Iron Giant
   A huge iron man appears from nowhere. He is so intent on listening and looking that he steps off a high cliff, scattering his body parts on the beach below. With the help of seagulls he puts himself back together and sets off looking for something to eat.

Activity Search the newspaper for articles or pictures of many types of robots. Compile a scrapbook of the items you find.

Chapter Two: The Return of the Iron Giant

Hogarth, a farmer's son, sees the giant and tells his father. Many of the other farmers don't believe in the giant until their farm machinery disappears and huge footprints are found. They dig a large pit and Hogarth lures the giant into the pit where the farmers cover him with earth.

Activity Modern Day Monsters: Do They Exist?

There are many who claim to have seen the monster named Bigfoot in the northern parts of the United States. Read the news article that follows. Give three reasons why it could be true and three reasons it could not be true.

"Wisconsin Tribune" Nov. 17, 1976

Bigfoot Gone, Rumors Linger

The Cashton Creature sighted by a local farmer one week ago is no where to be found and some believe that the hairy, seven-foot tall creature was an injured bear that was later killed by a hunter or hunters unknown. Cashton Police Chief said he has no report of a bear being shot. The Game Warden also said he had no reports. To have been shot legally the bear would have to have been taken with a bow and arrow. The use of a gun would subject the hunter to a fine.

One half mile from where the farmer spotted the smelly, hairy creature are several bee hives which were unmolested. Others believe the creature was a bear badly burned in a recent forest fire and the burns resulted in gangrene, accounting for the smell. Another rumor is that the creature is an escaped gorilla from a circus or zoo.

Another farmer and his son from Sparta were hiking in the woods last week and came across four footprints 18 inches long and seven inches wide. He attempted to make a cast of the footprint, but the cast broke and only crumbled pieces remain.

Chapter Three: What's To Be Done With the Iron Giant?

The Iron Giant pushes up out of the pit. The farmers don't know what to do to keep him from eating their machinery.

Activity

List your ideas on the lines in the box that follows. Score each idea **1** for **no, 2** for **maybe** and **3** for **yes**. Total the scores for each idea. The idea with the highest score would be the best idea to try.

IDEAS	FAST	SAFE	EFFECTIVE	TOTAL

Chapter Four: The Space Being and the Iron Giant

Astronomers gaze at a star that turns into a terrible creature. It rushes toward Earth and lands, covering all of Australia. The creature demands food and will eat any living thing. The people of the Earth deploy all of their weapons but none can destroy the creature. Hogarth asks the Iron Giant to help.

Activity Imagine that the Iron Giant visited your province or state for the first time. Fill in the blanks to complete the following story from the Iron Giant's point of view.

I have traveled through (state or province) _____
and let me tell you what I found. People here like to _____
_____ and I thought this was very
_____. I stopped at a farm to get something to eat,
but the strangest things I saw there were _____ and
_____. The landscape was_____
_____. While I was trudging
down the road I saw the strangest machine. It had _____
and it was _____.
When people caught a glimpse of me they _____ and
_____
If I ever return I want to take more time to see _____

Chapter Five: The Iron Giant's Challenge

The Iron Giant challenges the space creature to a test of strength. Three times the giant proposes to lie down on a bed of fire and three times the space creature must fly to the sun and feel its fire. The Iron Giant wins the contest and the space creature is sent to live inside the moon and sing a beautiful melody that will bring peace on Earth.

Activity Create a rock opera!

Pete Townshend has written a rock opera based on <u>The Iron Giant</u> and titled "The Iron Man." You may want to listen to it. It is available from Atlantic Records.

Follow the pattern below in completing the last verse to summarize the story of <u>The Iron Giant</u> and create your own rock opera. The verses can be chanted to any rock beat.

CHORUS: Giant, giant, not compliant
    This is the tale of the iron giant. (repeat)

VERSE: Walking out along the cliff
    Staring silent without speech
    Falling right off the edge
    Breaking apart on the beach

CHORUS: Run, run everybody run
    The giant's loose and having fun (repeat)

VERSE: Gobbling up all the fences
    Stumbling right into a hole
    Marching straight into town
    Eating through a metal pole

CHORUS: Friends, friends, we all are friends (repeat)
    But this isn't where the story ends

VERSE: Challenging then _____

    Glowing hot _____

    Conquering all _____

    Soothing now _____

CHORUS: This is a tale that you can't top
    Now it's time for us to stop.

Add new verses by following the pattern. Insert your verses in the order in which the action happened in the story

6. Research Topics

Research one of these important story topics. Choose one of the models to report your research findings. Present your report to the class.

Topics

Iron and/or Metals	Nobel Peace Prize Winners
Robots	Orion(Constellations)
Melting Points	Australia
Monsters	Black Holes
Quasars	Space Travel
Stars	Giant Creatures
Music That Soothes	Music Compositions About Space

Artists' Paintings of Monsters, Giants or the Universe
Poetry About Monsters, Giants, or the Universe

Ways to report research

Bio Poem

First name _____

Four Traits _____

Related to _____

Cares deeply about _____

Who feels _____

Who needs _____

Who gives _____

Who would like to see _____

Resident of _____

Fact and Fiction Book

On one page make a statement. Ask your reader to guess if it is fact or fiction.

On the next page state whether it is fact or fiction and tell why.

Illustrate your book.

Alliterative Report

If your topic begins with **R** (**Example** Robots) include the information you find in two or three alliterative paragraphs, as many words as possible beginning with the first letter of your topic.

Acrostic Poem

Summarize your topic as an acrostic poem. Keep note cards to show where you got your information.

Iron is refined into steel.
Rust-resistant iron contains chromium.
Other minerals are added.
Needing a blast furnace for smelting.

Write a Letter Report

Write a letter from one Nobel Peace Prize winner to another Nobel Peace Prize winner.

Your letter needs to give information about both and include some advice from one to the other.

INDUCTIVE REASONING The Drakenberg Adventure Lloyd Alexander. Dutton, 1988.

The Grand Duchess of the proud but poor Kingdom of Drakenberg invites 18 year old Vesper Holly and her Aunt and Uncle to the Diamond Jubilee celebration. . . but alas, it may be the final year of existence for Drakenberg. The country is so poor that it is about to be overtaken by a larger country.

Unfortunately, the sinister Dr. Helvitius, also arrives in Drakenberg with two objectives . . . to kill Vesper and her guardians and to bleed tiny Drakenberg of any treasures it might own. Vesper is determined to prevent Helvitius from stealing anything from Drakenberg and to find a way to save the small country from oblivion.

Activity

1. Work in groups of four. Each group member gets one clue card.
2. Clues must be shared orally. Notes can be taken.
3. By sharing clues can your group discover:
   A. What treasure did Dr. Helvitius find?
   B. How did he plan to get it out of the country?
   C. How did Vesper thwart Dr. Helvitius's plan?
   D. How did Drakenberg find income to survive?

CLUE CARD	CLUE CARD
In the Duchy of Drakenberg those who commit a crime must forfeit all of their property to the Duchy. Schwanfeld Castle's lands are rich in bauxite (aluminum) Dr. Helvitius has a special cheese barrel made with a false compartment.	Dr. Helvitius takes a barrel of cheese to the train station and pays to have it shipped to Carpathia, a neighboring kingdom. Dr. Helvitius is an art lover who would risk anything (even commit a crime) to own a valuable painting. Schwanfeld Castle and Drakenberg Palace are both located in the Duchy of Drakenberg.
CLUE CARD	**CLUE CARD**
Dr. Helvitius tricked the owner into selling him Schwanfeld Castle. The baggage handler switched the barrels. Vesper Holly bought a real cheese in an ordinary cheese barrel on the morning the train was to depart for Carpathia.	A fifteenth century Da Vinci painting was stored away in the cellar of Schwanfeld Castle and forgotten. It is a crime to remove art treasures from the Duchy of Drakenberg.

MORE VESPER HOLLY BOOKS

The El Dorado Adventure (Dutton, 1989)
Vesper sails to El Dorado to inspect a volcano she has inherited. The suave Alain de Rochefort is determined to acquire her property . . . and the fate of the last tribe of the Chirica Indians depends on whether or not he gets it. In the jungle Vesper faces deadly foes which seem to be two steps ahead of her and one step behind her.

The Illyrian Adventure (Dutton, 1986)
In the Land of Illyria, Vesper is caught in a struggle between two rebel forces.

The Jedera Adventure (Dutton, 1989)
Returning a library book is easy . . . unless the library is in North Africa and the book is in the hands of Vesper Holly!

The Philadelphia Adventure (Dutton, 1990)
Vesper is asked by President Grant to rescue two kidnaped children of a visiting diplomat . . . with the background of the Centennial Exposition in Philadelphia of 1876.

NANCY'S ALL TIME FAVORITE NOVELS

These novels get the M & M AWARD!

<u>M</u>agnificent stories and <u>M</u>emorable Characters

<u>The Best School Year Ever</u> by Barbara Robinson. HarperCollins, 1994.
  No one is immune from the Herdmans' pranks yet the meanest kids in town never seem to get caught. The problem begins when the teacher assigns a class project . . . everyone must come up with a compliment for a classmate . . . including the Herdmans.

<u>The BFG</u> by Roald Dahl. Farrar, 1982.
  Just imagine suddenly knowing you may be eaten for breakfast in the very near future. This is exactly what worries Sophie when she is snatched from her bed in the middle of the night by a giant with a stride as long as a tennis court. Luckily for Sophie, the BFG is far more jumbly than his disgusting neighbors, whose favorite pastime is guzzling and swallomping nice little children. Sophie is determined to stop all this so she and the BFG cook up a plan to rid the world of the trogglehumping, bogthumping giants forever!

<u>Beyond the Western Sea: Book One</u> by Avi. Orchard, 1996.
  It is 1851. Maura and Patrick O'Connell, fifteen and twelve-year-old Irish peasants, seek to escape a country destroyed by famine and the greed of English landlords. For Sir Laurence Kirkle, eleven and son of one such English lord, America holds the promise of justice, though he steals a fortune from his father to get there. How the O'Connells and young Laurence come to share a common fate in the English city of Liverpool, embarkation port for America, makes for an adventure alive with ironic coincidence and surprise.

<u>Blitzcat</u> by Robert Westall. Scholastic, 1989.
  The black cat travels through war time England in search of her master. She meets many people along the way from the deformed Stalker who becomes a hero to the frightened young machine gunner who takes comfort from the cat. A journey through Great Britain in World War II that is hard to interrupt.

<u>Charlie and the Chocolate Factory</u> by Roald Dahl. Knopf, 1973.
  A young boy lives with his parents and grandparents in a small house. They don't have very much money and he rarely gets to do exciting things – until one very exciting day. He is one out of five children to visit a chocolate factory where the world's most wonderful chocolate is made. What happens when he passes through the doors? What happens when one by one the children disappear?

<u>The Door in the Wall</u> by Marguerite deAngeli. Doubleday, 1949.
  Robin had to be brave when his father left to fight the Scots and when his mother was called away to care for the Queen. He was brave when he became sick and his legs would no longer hold him up or could even be felt. But, when the servants deserted him and he was left alone, he began to doubt how long he could hold on.
  Brother Luke saves his life, but Robin must face many problems and dangers. Is his father dead on the battlefield? Will his mother ever return and find him? What is to become of him without the use of his legs? How could he ever serve his king?

Harry Potter and the Sorcerer's Stone by J.K. Rowling. Scholastic, 1997.

Harry Potter has never been the star of a Quidditch team, scoring points while riding a broom far above the ground. He knows no spells, has never helped to hatch a dragon, and has never worn a cloak of invisibility. All he knows is a miserable life with the Dursleys, his horrible aunt and uncle, and their abominable son, Dudley, a great big swollen spoiled bully. Harry's room is in a tiny closet at the foot of the stairs, and he hasn't had a birthday party in eleven years.

But all that is about to change when a mysterious letter arrives by owl messenger. The letter is an invitation to an incredible place that Harry will find unforgettable. For it is at Hogwarts School of Witchcraft and Wizardry that Harry finds not only friends, aerial sports, and magic in everything from classes to meals, but a great destiny that's been waiting for him if he can survive the encounter.

The Haymeadow by Gary Paulsen. Delacorte Press, 1992.

At fourteen John Barron is asked, like his father and his father's father before him, to spend the summer taking care of their sheep in the haymeadow. Six thousand sheep, and John will be alone, except for two horses, four dogs, and all those sheep. John doesn't feel up to the task but he hopes against hope that if he can accomplish it, he will finally please his undemonstrative father. But John finds that the adage "things just happen to sheep" is true when the river floods, coyotes attack, and one dog's feet get cut. Through it all he relies on his own resourcefulness, ingenuity, and talents to try to get through.

Holes by Louis Sachar. Farrar, Straus & Giroux, 1998.

Stanley Yelnat's family has a history of bad luck, so he isn't too surprised when a miscarriage of justice sends him to a boy's juvenile detention center, Camp Green Lake. There is no lake, it has been dry for over a hundred years, and it's hardly a camp: as punishment, the boys must each dig a hole a day, five feet deep, five feet across, in the hard earth of the dried-up lake bed. The warden claims that this pointless behavior builds character, but that's a lie. Stanley must try to dig up the truth.

The Iron Giant: A Story In Five Nights by Ted Hughes. Faber & Faber, Ltd. 1985.

A mysterious creature stalks the land, eating barbed wire and devouring tractors and plows. The farmers are mystified and afraid. Then they glimpse him in the night: the Iron Giant, taller than a house, with glowing headlight eyes and an insatiable taste for metal. The hungry giant must be stopped at all costs.

Kneeknock Rise by Natalie Babbitt. Farrar, 1970.

The Mammoth Mountains are high enough to cast a dark shadow over the little village of Instep which served as a stage for the fearful events that happened. One would never want to climb these mountains for if you did you might meet the Megrimum! On any stormy night its anguished and despairing howls rolled down the mountain striking fear in the hearts of brave men and women alike. Yet the creature had for so long been a part of village life that the people would have missed it had it disappeared. So to keep it happy they held a fair each year and invited brave visitors to come and hear the creature's howls. Life might have gone on the way it always had if Egan had not come to visit his aunt and uncle. When he dared to poke fun at the idea of a monster on the mountain, he received a dare to climb the mountain and take a look.

Matilda by Roald Dahl. Puffin Books, 1988.

Matilda spoke clearly at the age of one and read all the works of Charles Dickens at the age of four. Were the Wormwoods pleased with their child's unusual abilities? Of course not! "You're spoiled," Mr. Wormwood screeched. "Why would you want a book when we have a perfectly fine telly?" Saying this, he grabbed her library book and ripped it to pieces

Matilda did not go to school until age five and a half because her parents forgot to enroll her. Her teacher was the smiley, huggy Miss Honey. It did not take Miss Honey long to discover how gifted Matilda was. She immediately reported this news to the headmistress, Miss Trunchbull. It is important to know that Miss Trunchbull was a kid-hating bully. Cross her and she would throw you right out the window. It would take a super human genius to get rid of her. And that, of course, is exactly what Matilda was a sweet, gentle, and crafty genius.

The Pushcart War by Jean Merrill. Harper & Row, 1964.

The Pushcart War started on the afternoon of March 15, 1976, when a truck ran down a pushcart belonging to a flower peddler. The pushcart was flattened and the owner of the pushcart was pitched head first into a pickle barrel. This was only the first incident in a war that lasted four months in the traffic-snarled streets of New York. The trucks had become so aggressive and reckless that the pushcart peddlers had no choice but to fight back. Under the leadership of Maxie Hammerman, the Pushcart King, they developed a strategy to outwit the truckers and the corrupt politicians who backed them. The use of a secret weapon, a modified pea shooter, was crucial to the strategy. Finally, when a movie star, the children of New York and the general public got involved, the truckers were in more trouble than ever expected.

The Righteous Revenge of Artemis Bonner by Walter Dean Myers. HarperCollins, 1992.

In 1880 two important events took place. Catfish Grimes shot dead Ugly Ned Bonner, Uncle to Artemis Bonner and Artemis headed west to avenge Uncle Ugly's death and find the gold mine left to him in his uncle's will. Catfish Grimes is determined not to be caught. He would also like to find the gold mine before Artemis does. But Artemis has the strength of true determination! He tracks Catfish from Mexico to Alaska and back again. Finally they meet in a shootout in front of the Bird Cage Saloon. Catfish yelled, "When I count three go for your gun." No sooner had he shouted "one!" than both Catfish and Artemis drew.

The Snow Goose by Paul Gallico. Random House reissue, 1988.

Philip Rhayader, a hunchback, retreats to an isolated lighthouse where he paints and cares for wild things. Twelve-year-old Frith brings a wounded snow goose to Philip and he heals the bird, gaining its trust as well as that of the girl. Over a ten-year period Frith and Philip are friends, she coming to the lighthouse when the bird is there. Too late she realizes her love for the gentle Philip as he sails to Dunkirk to rescue men trapped on the beaches in World War II.

Stone Fox by John Gardiner. HarperCollins, 1980.

Little Willy was worried. Not just a little bit worried like when he overslept that one morning and found the chickens had eaten his breakfast, but a lot worried. The worry began the morning grandfather would not get out of bed. Grandfather was usually the first one up and had half the farm chores done before Willy stirred. On the morning grandfather did not get up, Willy was so worried that he ran to get the doctor. She gave grandfather a real thorough examination but could find nothing wrong with him. "Some folks just decide to stop living," she said, "and there is not much anyone can do about it until they change their minds." The tax man talked about selling the farm for back taxes. "But we always pay the bills on time," Willy protested. "Not the tax bills," the tax man replied. "You owe ten years' back taxes. That comes to about five hundred dollars." Grandfather couldn't help. He just laid in bed and stared at the ceiling. How was Willy going to raise five hundred dollars?

The True Confessions of Charlotte Doyle by Avi. Orchard, 1990.

The year was 1832 when 13-year old Charlotte Doyle discovered she was the only passenger on the Seahawk setting sail from Liverpool, England to Providence Rhode Island. She was astonished to find her cabin so small, dark, and inhabited by crawly things. A visit by the ship's cook warned her of the cruelty of the Captain and gave her a knife for protection. On this fateful journey she would see a man whipped and flogged and she herself would be accused of murder. Charlotte bravely promised herself she would not succumb to her feelings of despair. She would survive this voyage and all its horrors.

The Whipping Boy by Sid Fleischman. Greenwillow, 1986.

He is known throughout the land as Prince Brat, a name he justly deserves! In his kingdom it is forbidden to spank the heir to the throne. So an orphan named Jemmy is plucked from the streets to serve as a whipping boy.

Jemmy dreams of running away but finds himself saddled with the prince who is a less than desirable companion. Captured by cutthroats, Jemmy plans the prince's rescue, which the prince refuses to accept. He likes the adventure of being a prisoner!

Escaping from thieves, bears, rats and other dangers, the two boys survive and the lives of both are changed forever.

The Wolves of Willoughby Chase by Joan Aiken. Doubleday, 1962.

Wicked wolves without and a grim governess within the great English country house of Willoughby Chase prove sore trials to brave and determined Bonnie, her cousin Sylvia, and their faithful friend, Simon. Little did the girls dream, when Bonnie's parents left them in the care of the terrible Miss Slighcarp, what the future would hold. Their life at the Chase seemed almost unendurable but then Miss Slighcarp sent them off to her sister, brutal Mrs. Brisket, and her daughter, the awful Diana. With only Simon to help them, Bonnie and Sylvia face many chilly moments in this tale of adventure and suspense.

WHAT CAN YOU DO WITH A POEM?

WHAT RESEARCH SAYS:

The most successful way to enlist children's enthusiasm for poetry is to get them involved in "doing a poem". - Nancy Larrick

Research shows that neurological impressioning is a proven method for helping children acquire the patterns of language. - Dr. Jane Healy

Of 132 fifth grade students taught poetry combined with music, 87% wanted to study poems with music the next year and 85% thought that studying poetry with music helped them to learn new things. - Demetrales, P. Lehigh University, 1986.

The sharing of poetry should be active, not passive. Students should be encouraged to sing or chant the poems, add additional words or sounds, and/or illustrate their favorite poems using them as models for their own poetry writing.

Read aloud to rhythm music. (Any march or waltz tune.)

Herman found a big dead bug
Sister put it in the trash,
But before the trash is burned,
Herman wants his bug returned.

A boy named Les
Was such a mess
His stringy hair was everywhere
And then one day his mom was firm
Gave Les a girly, curly perm.

Jack McFee caught a bee
Sitting in his big back porch.
Was it Jack or was the bee
Sitting there for all to see?

Elaborate on the poem. Add words or sounds.

After each line of the poem, add an appropriate word or sound.
The word or sound can be softly chanted as each line of the poem is read.

Herman found a big dead bug	(Look! Look! Look! Look!
Sister put it in the trash,	There it goes! There it goes!
But before the trash is burned,	Sizzle, sizzle, sizzle, sizzle
Herman wants his bug returned.	Yeah! Yeah! Yeah! Yeah!

SHARED READING: POETRY

1. Read it aloud.

2. Read a line and have students echo the line.

3. Divide the class into two groups. Groups read aloud alternate lines.

4. Underline key words, write to the side of each line and create a much shorter version of the poem.

5. Elaborate: what words, phrases can be added after each line for students to say and demonstrate.

6. Make an overhead transparency of the poem. Teacher and students read it aloud together

7. Read the poem to rhythm music. Read aloud with soft mood music in the background.

8. Try singing the poem to the tune of "The Yellow Rose of Texas."

9. Add new verses.

Mr. Picket
by Nancy Polette

Mr. Picket picked a pocket
And he got a baked potato
So he walked to town to trade it
For a juicy ripe tomato.

Mr. Picket picked a pocket
And he got a shiny nickel
So he ran to town to trade it
For a sour green dill pickle.

Mr. Picket picked a pocket
And he got a kitty cat
So he flew to town to trade it
For a brand new tall top hat.

Mr. Picket picked a pocket
And he got a trap for mice
It was then that he decided
Picking pockets wasn't nice.

Your turn. Follow the pattern.

Mr. Picket picked a pocket

And he got

_____

So he _____ to town

to trade it

For a _____

Mr. Picket picked a pocket

And he got

_____

So he _____ to town

to trade it

For a _____

ECHO READING

The value of this kind of chiming comes from the children hearing themselves "reading" with the poise and cadence of the mature reader. Any reader having trouble creating the sound-of-sense can be helped by echo readings such as "The Bear Song." Let's echo!

THE BEAR SONG

You read:
   The other day
   I met a bear
   out in the woods
   a way out there.

Children echo:
   The other day
   I met a bear
   out in the woods
   a way out there.

Read together
   The other day I met a bear
   out in the woods a way out there.

   out in the woods
   a way out there.

   out in the woods
   a way out there.

He looked at me.
I looked at him.
He sized me up.
I sized up him.

He looked at me.
I looked at him.
He sized me up.
I sized up him.

Read together
   He looked at me, I looked at him.
   He sized me up, I sized up him.

He sized me up.
I sized up him.
He said to me,
"Why don't you run?
I see you ain't
 got any gun."

He sized me up.
I sized up him.
He said to me,
"Why don't you run?
I see you ain't
got any gun."

Read together
   He said to me, "Why don't you run?
   I see you ain't got any gun."

"I see you ain't
got any gun."

"I see you ain't
got any gun."

I said to him,
"That's a good idea,"
so come on feet,
let's up and fleet."

I said to him,
"That's a good idea,"
so come on feet,
  let's up and fleet."

Read together
   I said to him, "That's a good idea,
   so come on feet, let's up and fleet."

"so come on feet,
let's up and fleet."

"so come on feet,
  let's up and fleet."

— an old song, author unknown

POEMS FOR TWO VOICES

SHOPPING SPREE

I'll take that lion with the curly mane   (Comb and brush, comb and brush)
An American Flyer railroad train   (Toot, chug. Toot, chug)
A rocking horse, a teddy bear,   (Cuddle up, cuddle up)
That great big bass drum over there.   (BOOM, BOOM, BOOM, BOOM!)
For shorter trips I'll take a scooter,   (Down the street, down the street)
And yes, throw in that new computer.   (Beep, beep, beep, beep)
What? You said it's not all free?   What? You said it's not all free?
I don't like this shopping spree.   I don't like this shopping spree.

THE THREE LITTLE PIGS: A POEM FOR TWO VOICES

Voice One	Voice Two
Three little pigs set out one day	
In the world to make their way	
Built with straw and sticks and bricks	
	Wolf was up to his old tricks.
	Blew out the window and the door
	Then turned around
	And blew some more.
Frightened pigs they ran away	
To their brother's home to stay	Could not blow the brick house down
Pigs rejoiced and went to town.	
	Said Wolf, retreating in the wood,
	"I'll go and eat Red Riding Hood."

POETRY AND ART Find pictures of famous paintings to match these poems. Look for other poems and paintings that go together.

WINDY NIGHTS

Whenever the moon and stars are set,
Whenever the wind is high,
All night long in the dark and wet,
  A man goes riding by.
Late in the night when the fires are out,
Why does he gallop and gallop about?
               R.L . Stevenson

PETS

Oh lady, dear lady
Watch out for your pets!
The keepers are coming
With butterfly nets.
"Where can you hide them?"
"Not here and not there!"
Let the dear little creatures
Hide in your hair.
            N. Polette

READING ALOUD WITH THREE VOICES

Find two other people. Read the poem. All read at the same time but each person reads a different verse.

THE PARADE

(Find 2 other people and read each verse separately, then all three verses at the same time)

Thump, boom! Thump, boom!
Thump, boom! Move over make room!
Thump, boom! Thump, boom!
Thump, boom! Move over make room!
What? You don't like all the noise we have made?
Then this is the end of our great big parade.

Left, right, it's a glorious sight
High stepping, wide stepping, morning till night.
Left, right, it's a glorious sight
High stepping, wide stepping, morning till night.
What? You don't like all the noise we have made?
Then this is the end of our great big parade.

The twirlers are twirling, their banners unfurling
They're twisting and turning and leading the band
The twirlers are twirling, their banners unfurling
They're twisting and turning and leading the band
What? You don't like all the noise we have made?
Then this is the end of our great big parade.

READ TO MUSIC

Choose a favorite poem. Find music that fits the mood of the poem (happy, sad, tranquil, scary. Read the poem with music in the background.

SCARED

I'm scared of people six feet tall
And bugs that crawl up on the wall.
I don't care much for loud machines,
dark and creepy TV scenes,
spider webs, and doors that lock
or the bully on the block.
But when I grow to six feet three
Someone might be scared of me!

POETRY PATTERN BOOK REPORTS

The poetry patterns on this page are all used to describe a character or scene from a favorite book. Use one of the patterns in reporting about a book you have read.

FIVE SENSES POEM
Line

1-Color	War is brown
2-Sound	It sounds like thunder
3-Taste	It tastes like bitter grapes
4-Smell	It smells like yesterday's garbage
5-Sight	It looks like an ancient ruin
6-Feeling	It makes you feel like crying

Hiroshima No Pika
by Toshi Maruki

PHONE NUMBER POEM
Each line has number of syllables in a chosen phone number

3 Old houses
3 With etched paint
4 Live lonely lives
7 Waiting to be occupied
5 Perhaps tomorrow
6 And the only sound heard
5 Was yesterday's ghost
Who Knew There'd Be Ghosts?
by Bill Brittain

BUILD A NAME POETRY
Twelve o'clock
And
Time to escape
The changing that will
Earn her dream
Running faster and faster
Cinderella escapes
Only to return
Again
To
Sitting alone by the fire
Tattercoats by Joseph Jacobs

TERSE VERSE
What Alexander said about

the day	Gray Day
the ride	Tight Flight
the lunch	Drag Bag
his pajamas	

_____

dinner

_____

dentist

_____

TV

_____

Alexander And The Terrible Horrible No Good Very Bad Day by Judith Viorst

BIO POEM
Line

1	First name	Gretel
2	Four traits	Small, lost, tired, hungry
3	Related to	Sister of Hansel
4	Cares deeply about	Cares deeply about her family
5	Who feels	Who feels afraid
6	Who needs	Who needs a place to sleep
7	Who gives	Who gives companionship
8	Who fears	Who fears the witch
9	Who would like to see	Who would like to see her father again
10	Resident of	Resident of the forest

Hansel and Gretel

ADVERB POETRY

1	Adverb	Humbly
2	Adverb	Hopefully
3	Adverb	Honestly
4	Noun	The man
5	Verb	Pleads
6	Noun with description	To the wrathful king
7	Noun	Water!

The King's Fountain by Lloyd Alexander

POETRY PROBLEM SOLVING

Most of Mother Goose's family had problems. Humpty Dumpty couldn't be put together again. Mary's garden would not grow. Little Bo Peep lost her sheep and Miss Muffet was afraid of the spider.

1. Choose a Mother Goose rhyme.
>Old Mother Goose
>When she wanted to wander
>Would fly through the air
>On a very fine gander

2. Decide what the problem is.

Traveling on a gander would be difficult in rain or snow,

3. Write a second verse to solve the problem.

>Except in the snow
>Or the sleet or the rain
>When she traveled first class
>On a jumbo jet plane. (From <u>Flying With Mother Goose</u> by Nancy Polette)

TRY THIS ONE

>Humpty Dumpty sat on a wall
>Humpty Dumpty had a great fall
>All the king's horses and all the king's men
>Couldn't put Humpty together again.

What is the problem?

_____

_____

_____

Write a two line solution to the problem.
Example   Along came a teacher and with much ado
             Put Humpty together with thumbtacks and glue. (From <u>Flying With Mother
                                      Goose</u> by Nancy Polette)

_____

_____

_____

WRITING POETRY: PATTERNS FROM THE MASTERS

Who has seen the wind?
Neither you nor I
But when the trees bow down their heads (personification)
The wind is passing by.
                                    - Christina Rosetti

Who has seen the _____ (desert, mountain, ocean)

Only _____ or _____

But when _____ (use personification)

The _____

Hold fast to dreams
For if dreams die
Life is a broken-winged bird
That cannot fly.
                                    - Langston Hughes

Hold fast to _____ (name a value)

For if _____ _____(synonym for fade away)

Life is a _____ (metaphor)

That_____

Other Poetry Patterns

Swift things are beautiful
Swallows and deer
And lightning that falls
Bright-veined and clear
And slow things are beautiful
The closing of day
The pause of a wave
That curves downward to spray.
            - Elizabeth Coatsworth

Out in the woods
The pine trees wear
Soft white capes
In the clear cold air
And look like princes standing there.
                        - Anonymous

LEARNING ABOUT A POET: EMILY DICKINSON

Emily Dickinson was a lively young girl. She loved parties and skating and life in general. She fell in love at age 18 but never married. She became a recluse refusing to leave her home. She had very few acquaintances and spent her days writing poetry. She loved children and would leave baskets of cookies for them but never left her house to speak to them. She remained a recluse until she died at age 54.

Underline words in this poem students don't know. Look them up! Now does the poem make more sense?

"There is no frigate like a book to take us lands away,
Nor any coursers like a page of prancing poetry.
This traverse may the poorest take without oppress of toll,
How frugal is the chariot that bears the human soul."

- Emily Dickinson

Paragraph Challenge
Use any words underlined in the poem in a paragraph describing Emily Dickinson's life.

Using the Poet's Tools Personification

Frequently the woods are pink,
Frequently are brown.
Frequently the hills undress (personification)
Behind my native town. (Emily Dickinson)

Choose something familiar in nature. Follow the pattern of the Dickinson poem to write about it.

Frequently _____

Frequently _____

Frequently _____

_____

FINDING A POEM IN A POEM

No need to find the perfect word for a poem - just use the words you find. Poetry may be found in newspaper articles, ads, the telephone directory, labels, informational writing or any form of prose. It may also be found in poetry. The example below is "found" in Robert Louis Stevenson's poem, The Wind. Just take one or two words from each line to create a new poem. Capitalization and punctuation may be altered. From Robert Louis Stevenson's Child's Garden of Verses.

The Wind	Wind
I saw you toss the kites on high	The kites
And blow the birds about the sky.	blow about the sky.
And all around I heard you pass,	I heard you!
Like ladies' skirts across the grass-	like
O wind, a-blowing all day long,	wind
O wind that sings so loud a song!	that sings.
I saw the different things you did,	I saw you!
But always you yourself you hid.	I felt you!
I felt you push, I heard you call,	All
I could not see yourself at all-	day long,
O wind, a-blowing all day long,	so loud!
O wind, that sings so loud a song!	
O you that are so strong and cold,	So strong
O blower, are you young or old?	are you!
Are you a beast of field and tree,	Beast!
Or just a stronger child than me?	Stronger than me!
O wind, a-blowing all day long,	O wind,
O wind, that sings so loud a song!	so loud.

FOUND POETRY IN PROSE

"There you are!" cried Toad. "There's the real life for you embodied in that little cart. The open road, the dusty highway, the heath, the common, the hedgerows, the rolling downs!! Camps, villages, towns, cities! Here today, up and off to somewhere else tomorrow. Travel, change, interest, excitement! The whole world before you and a horizon always changing!"

These are the words of Toad from <u>The Wind in the Willows</u> when he falls in love with a motor car. It is fun to look at a paragraph of prose and spot the key words which can be rearranged to create a poem

> **A traveling cart**
> **An eager toad**
> **Motoring down the open road**
> **Highways, commons, rolling downs,**
> **Towns and cities, laughing clowns,**
> **Here today and gone tomorrow,**
> **The traveler's life is joy, not sorrow.**

"Glorious, stirring sight, the poetry of motion! The REAL way to travel. The ONLY way to travel. Villages skipped, towns and cities jumped, always somebody else's horizon! What a flowery track lies before me. What dust clouds shall spring up behind me as I speed on my reckless way. That swan! That sunbeam! That Thunderbolt! O Bless! O my! O my!"

Note key words and rearrange them to create your poem.

_____

_____

_____

_____

_____

POETRY CHARACTERS

It is fun to describe characters by comparing them to things we meet and use everyday. Follow these directions to describe a favorite character.

1. List things found in a particular place (like a kitchen or a garden) or on an object (like a car or clothing).

oven	shirt	steering wheel	hoe
bowl	button	engine	hose
pitcher	sleeve	wheels	flower
cabinet	collar	seat	seeds
blender	hat	clutch	weed
cup	cuff	chassis	spade
teapot	scarf	brake	trowel
refrigerator	pants	toaster	cloak

2. Add to this list of human qualities and feelings. Describe a favorite character.

Examples

WHO IS SHE?

A bowlful of common sense
A cup of laughter
A pitcher filled with friendliness
A cabinet of determination.
                    (Dorothy)

WHO IS HE?

He steers through life
On a seat of humanity
In a chassis of tears
Clutching every opportunity
To put the brakes on human harm
Ever guarding the key
To the engine of compassion.
                    (Tinman)

RECIPE FOR A QUIDDITCH PLAYER

1 cup talented Quidditch player
2 tablespoons of courage
½ cup of determination
1 slice Hogwarts School application
2 large packages bumps and bruises
Mix Quidditch player with
    Opposing team
Fly for six hours, testing Nimbus
Remove the Snitch from play
Preserve Harry Potter as the best
 team Seeker and Quidditch winner
    ever!

Write a recipe for friendship,
 teamwork or Hogwarts School

RESEARCH RIDDLE POEMS

Here are ways to report research on a topic. Can you find the answers to complete the two riddle poems? Select another topic related to a story. Write a riddle poem about it.

A DICKENS RIDDLE POEM

Through Charles Dickens' looking

glasses We see the life of the lower

(1)_____ his (2)_____ novels

brought to life   (How Many?)

Orphans, prisons and social strife.

He wrote about a funny 'feller'

In <u>Pickwick Papers</u> named (3)____ ____

In <u>David Copperfield</u> did Dickens tell

of (4)_____ _____, a ne'er do well.

In <u>A Tale of Two Cities</u> there was a

sad solution

For lovers caught up in the (5)___ ___.

In <u>Oliver Twist</u> he writes of a time

that (6)_____ led boys to a life of

crime.

In Great Expectations, Pip would like

to throw daggers

At the silence of the Lawyer

(7)_____.

A Dickens' novel is the best read in town,

If you open one up, you can't put it

down.

Key: 1. classes 2. fifteen 3. Sam Weller
4. Wilkens Micwaber 5. French
Revolution 6. Fagan 7. Jaggers

A TITANIC RIDDLE POEM

Many wanted to make the first trip

on the (1) ____, the world's largest ship.

Into the facts we now will delve

Of this ship that sailed in (2)_____.

From Great Britain to (3)___ ___ _____.

The passengers we all must pity.

The Titanic was all of (4)____ feet long

"Nothing" they said, "could ever go

wrong."

There were (5)_____ souls on board

When a (6)_____ foot gash in its side

was gored.

By an (7) _____ during a lookout's lull,

It ripped and tore right through the

(8)_____.

'Run for the lifeboats!' No smile and no

laugh,

But the boats had room for only (9) __.

The number of people rescued alive

Was roughly (10)_____.

The builders, they were wrong, we think

To claim this huge ship would not sink.

Key: 1. Titanic 2. 1912 3. New York City
4. 882.5 5. 2200 6. 300 7. iceberg
8. hull 9. half 10. 705

READERS THEATRE

Readers theatre is beneficial to all readers. The student who does not read well need lots of practice. Dialogue is much easier to read than narrative. Students who do read well learn to slow down, read with expression and interpret the text.

FOUR TYPES OF SCRIPTS

1. Scripts to read as they are written.

2. Scripts to elaborate upon. Additional words or sounds can be added at the end of lines to liven up the script and make it more fun to perform and listen to.

3. Scripts which need additional material added. At specific places in the script the student is given a writing assignment. When the play is read, each writer reads what he or she has written at the appropriate point in the play.

4. Scripts that turn narrative into dialogue. Any text can become a readers theatre script by following simple directions given in this section for turning narrative into dialogue.

STAGING READERS THEATRE

The readers are usually arranged in a straight line with characters seated and narrators standing. The narrator for the protagonist stands next to the protagonist and the narrator for the antagonist stands next to the antagonist. In a three person script, the main character can be seated and the narrators are standing. If there is only one narrator, the narrator can be seated with characters standing on either side.

All characters carry and use scripts even if lines have been memorized although memorizing lines is NOT necessary. Characters who are not reading can look down or turn slightly away. When entering and taking their places on the "stage," readers carry the script in the hand which is away from the audience.

In practice sessions the readers should work on clear speech and on projecting the voice so that all can hear. Expressive and energetic reading should be practiced.

The cast should enter the stage or readers' area from two sides with each side entering at the same time. Posture should be good and the readers might indicate through body language the mood of the piece or something about the characters (are they energetic, tired, happy, sad, scared etc.?) At the conclusion of the performance the readers should bow together and exit in the appropriate mood.

THE LION AND THE MOUSE Adapted from Aesop's Fables

Reading Parts: Narrator One, Narrator Two, Lion, Mouse

NARRATOR ONE: It was a summer sunflower day. The rays of the sun spread out like petals of a flower to touch every part of the green meadow.

NARRATOR ONE: Little mouse peeked out from under a juniper bush, blinked his eyes at the bright light and called to his mouse friends.

MOUSE: What a beautiful day! What a glorious day! Come out, come out, come out and play.

NARRATOR TWO: Just then a huge, furry paw reached out. The huge, furry paw caught mouse and lifted him up and up until mouse was looking right into the mouth of a lion!

MOUSE: Please, Sir Lion, mice are not tasty. Mice are not flavorful. Mice are not served in the best restaurants. Mice are not good to eat at all. And besides, if you let me go, perhaps I can help you some day.

LION: HO, HO, HO! You help me, the King of all the beasts? Never! But I admire one who is brave enough to stand up to the king so I will let you go. Just don't come by my way again. I might make a meal of you yet.

NARRATOR ONE: So mouse went on his way and months passed until one day mouse woke up in his hidey hole in the meadow. It was a frosty, tickle-your nose autumn day.

NARRATOR TWO: Mouse called to his mouse friends.

MOUSE: What a beautiful day! What a glorious day! Come out, come out, come out and play.

NARRATOR TWO: Instead of the squeaky squeaks of mice, little mouse heard another sound. It was a strange sound. It was a scary sound.

LION: (slowly) OHHHHH! OHHHHH!

NARRATOR ONE: Little mouse crawled out from under the juniper bush and looked up, down and all around. A big, brown, furry mountain had grown up overnight like a giant mushroom after a rain. But the big brown furry mountain was covered by a net. Then it moved!

NARRATOR TWO: Mouse blinked and looked again. It was not a furry mountain. It was lion caught in a net.

MOUSE: Good morning, Sir Lion. If you will stop thrashing about, I believe my friends and I can help you escape.

NARRATOR ONE: Lion stopped thrashing about. He listened as mouse gave three loud squeaks, an SOS in mouse language.

NARRATOR TWO: The mice set to work gnawing on the ropes until there was a hole large enough to free the lion. Then the mice disappeared as quickly as they had come, all except for little mouse.

LION: Little mouse, I am forever in your debt, not only for freeing me but for teaching me a most important lesson.

ENTIRE CAST: Little friends can be as helpful as big friends.

Authoring A CHINESE CINDERELLA adapted by Nancy Polette

Here is another version of the Cinderella tale. Parts of the story are missing! Either working alone or in small groups, complete the missing parts (these are the parts marked AUDIENCE). You will have to use many thinking skills . . . fluency, flexibility, originality, elaboration, forecasting, decision-making, problem solving and evaluation. When the story has been completed, perform it for other classes in your school.

MOTHER: (To audience) Let me tell you how this tale begins. I was a widow with two daughters of my own when I married a wealthy mandarin who was a widower with one daughter. Well, I thought, you take the bad with the good. I could put up with his daughter (even though she was more beautiful than my own). I would just ignore her.

SISTERS: And then our wealthy stepfather died leaving his daughter, Shih Chieh, in our home. But we thought of a way to get rid of her! "Mother," we said, "Give her the most dangerous jobs you can think of. The village would not criticize you for expecting a dutiful daughter to work."

MOTHER: (To the audience) Give me some dangerous jobs for Shih Chieh to do. The riskier the better! Ha Ha Ha Ha Ha!

AUDIENCE: Give several dangerous jobs.

SHIH CHIEH: Oh, how shall I ever retrieve stepmother's ring from the bottom of this deep pond? My net is not long enough. But look! There is a fish in my net. It is the most beautiful fish I have ever seen!

AUDIENCE: Describe the fish.

SHIH CHIEH: Dear fish, your beauty overwhelms me. Each morning I shall bring you scraps from my plate and we shall become great friends.

SISTERS: Mother! See what Shih Chieh does! She feeds scraps to a fish in the pond and then she talks to it. Isn't that stupid!

MOTHER: We shall give her even less to eat then. And I shall put a stop to those visits. Bring me a knife.

SISTERS: Listen to us, Shih Chieh, there is no more fish for you to talk to. Mother slit its belly open and buried its bones in the field. Now where are you running off to? Crying won't bring it back.

WISE WOMAN: Do not fear Shih Chieh. No one can see me but you. Dry your tears and go to the field where the bones are buried. Touch the ground and make a wish and it shall be yours.

SHIH CHIEH: If this is true I shall wait until stepmother has taken my sisters off to the festival. I should like to go too, for the Emperor will be there, therefore, I shall wish for:

AUDIENCE: Name her wishes. All wishes should have to do with the things she will need to attend the festival.

SISTERS: Oh, look! Our gowns are far better than any others here, The Emperor will surely dance with one of us first. But look! Who is that stranger? The Emperor is approaching her. He is leading her into the dancing circle. Quick, let us do something to get his attention!

AUDIENCE: Tell what the sisters do.

MOTHER: Foolish daughters! I could have told you that would not work. But wait, that strange girl looks exactly like Shih Chieh!

SHIH CHIEH: (Speaks to audience) Oh, dear, Stepmother has seen me. I must flee. If I am back at the cottage before her she may think she was mistaken.

EMPEROR: Where are you going? Come back! Guards, catch that girl! You fools, how could you have let her get away?

GUARD: In her haste she lost this golden slipper. Perhaps if we search the village we shall find her.

EMPEROR: There must be a better way to find her. Perhaps the audience has some ideas. There must be many wise people here. Tell me, what shall we do?

AUDIENCE: Give the Emperor ideas for finding Shih Chieh.

EMPEROR: Good. We will place the slipper in a pavilion near where it was lost. The maiden who places its mate beside it will be the one I seek.

GUARD: Three days have passed and only the curious have come to look. Look at that girl. She is hiding something under her cloak. Stop thief! Give me that slipper you have stolen.

EMPEROR: She is not a thief. See the slipper is still in its place, She has the missing slipper. Come with me to the palace, beautiful lady, and your every wish will be granted.

SHIH CHIEH: I cannot, kind sir, for I must stay in the village where I shall be needed to:

AUDIENCE: List all of the ways Shih Chieh will help the village.

MOTHER & SISTERS: We will come to the palace. After all, we gave Shih Chieh food and shelter all these years. Have we not earned a special palace room for our trouble?

EMPEROR: This is true. A special room has been reserved for you. It is . . .

AUDIENCE: Tell what the room is and what they will do there.

ENTIRE CAST: And Shih Chieh returned to the village were she was much loved for her good works and the stepmother and stepsisters lived unhappily ever after!

Authoring Tattercoats Collected and edited by Joseph Jacobs

Illustrated by Margot Tomes. G. P. Putnam's, 1989.

Here is the jacket copy turned into a play. What words or sounds can you add to make the performance livelier or more interesting?

Speaking Parts: Narrator One, Narrator Two, Gooseherd, The Old Lord, Tattercoats, The Stranger, King

Narrator 1:	In a palace by the sea an old Lord
Lord:	sat day after day.
Narrator 1:	His white beard
Lord:	grew so long
Narrator 1:	that it tangled around his chair. He was all alone
Lord:	except for servants and a granddaughter
Narrator 1:	he hated bitterly, for her mother, his only daughter had died at her birth.
Narrator 2:	So the child grew up with no one to care for her (Tattercoats: and was given only scraps from the kitchen and clothes from the rag bag.
Narrator 2:	But when she grew sad she had only
Tattercoats:	to find the gooseherd boy who would play on his pipes
Gooseherd:	and cheer her up.
Narrator 1:	Now it happened that the King
King:	was to give a great ball and from the ladies attending would find a bride for the Prince.
Narrator 2:	The gooseherd proposed that
Gooseherd:	they go together to see the fine palace.
Narrator 2:	As they were piping along the way, a well-dressed stranger
Stranger:	joined them.
Narrator 1:	The more the pipes were played, the more he
Stranger:	fell in love with Tattercoats.
Narrator 1:	The stranger begged her
Stranger:	to come to the ball
Narrator 2:	but in her tattered clothes she
Tattercoats:	dared not do so.
Narrator 1:	But the pipes of the gooseherd
Gooseherd:	that could cheer her and wipe away her tears
Narrator 1:	had other magic as well.
Narrator2:	And at the ball there will be some unexpected surprises as Tattercoats and the stranger
Tattercoats:	meet once again.

Authoring **THE BELL OF ATRI** an old tale adapted by Nancy Polette

What words, phrases or sounds can you add to the play to make it livelier or more interesting?

Speaking Parts: Narrator One, Narrator Two, Villagers (as many as desired), The Donkey, The Mean Man

Narrator One:	In the mountains of Italy is a small village with a magnificent bell. Now the villagers usually
Villagers:	get along with each other quite well,
Narrator Two:	but should a wrong be done, the person
Villagers:	who has been wronged has merely to ring the bell.
Narrator One:	Hearing the bell, the villagers
Villagers:	all gather around to decide what can be done to right the wrong.
Narrator Two:	After many years, the rope on the bell rotted away and the villagers
Villagers:	sent away for a very long rope.
Narrator One:	It must be long enough for the smallest person to reach.
Narrator Two:	Until the long rope arrived, a long vine was cut and attached to the bell.
Narrator One:	Now just outside the village lived
Mean Man:	a mean man.
Narrator Two:	His faithful donkey
Donkey:	who had worked hard and served him for many years (hee haw)
Narrator Two:	was his only companion. But the donkey
Donkey:	was old and could no longer work
Narrator One:	so the man
Mean Man:	beat him and chased him away.
Narrator Two:	As the donkey
Donkey:	wandered into town (clippity clop)
Narrator Two:	what did he find but
Donkey:	a delicious vine waiting to be eaten.
Narrator Two:	As the donkey nibbled the vine the bell began to ring.
Villagers:	"The donkey has been wronged!"
Narrator One:	the villagers cried, seeing how old and thin the poor beast was.
Villagers:	"The wrong must be righted!"
Narrator One:	And the mean man
Mean Man:	was brought to town and ordered
Villagers:	to put aside half of his gold for the care of the donkey
Narrator Two:	who, for the rest of his days
Donkey:	had a warm stall and plenty to eat.

Authoring THE MAGICIAN'S HELPER adapted by Nancy Polette

A play to write and read for primary grades. Each writing group should read the play through before writing its part. The group chooses someone to read what was written when that part of the play is reached.

MOTHER: My son Fritz is always causing trouble.

WRITER 1: **Tell all of the ways a curious boy can get into trouble.**

MOTHER: It is time you left home to make your own living.

FRITZ: Look at this long list of jobs. Let's see if I can find one I like.

WRITER 2: **List all of the jobs that Fritz sees on the list.**

FRITZ: I will be a magician's helper. That will be fun.

WRITER 3: **List what a magician's helper would do.**

NARRATOR: Fritz went to the castle of the magician and became his helper.

WRITER 4: **List some jobs that a magician's helper would do.**

FRITZ: I did not know I would have to carry water up these steps every day.

This is a hard job.

MAGICIAN: I have to leave for a short time. Get more water from the well and do not

touch any of my things.

FRITZ: He is gone. I will say magic words to the broom and it can carry the water for me.

NARRATOR: Fritz said the magic words he had heard the magician say.

WRITER 5: **Write the magic words.**

FRITZ: Stop, broom! That is too much water. Stop or I will take an ax and cut you into pieces.

NARRATOR: The broom did not stop so Fritz took an ax and cut it to pieces.

FRITZ: Oh, look! Each piece grows into a new broom. Now many brooms are carrying water.

WRITER 6: **Tell what the workshop looks like with water everywhere.**

NARRATOR: Before long the magician returned and found his workshop full of water.

MAGICIAN: Water here, water there, water, water everywhere. Did you do this, Fritz?

FRITZ: Yes, Sir. I put a spell on the broom but did not know how to turn it off. Shall I leave now?

MAGICIAN: You may stay but first you must . . .

WRITER 7: **Tell what Fritz must do for the magician.**

ENTIRE CAST: And from this day on you must only look and NEVER TOUCH!

Authoring DANGER IN OZ

Wizard:"Oh say can you see, Land of Oz is for me."

Dorothy:That's the Wizard you hear singing. He's looking through an old battered trunk he keeps in his room. I've often wondered what it is he treasures so much.

Writer One: Name things that could be in the Wizard's trunk.

Wizard: This may look like junk, but these are the things that have protected the Emerald City in the past. Unfortunately, once used, they cannot be used again.

Dorothy: Then he winked at me. He said if I'd keep an eye out for intruders, he'd let me . . .

Writer Two: What would the Wizard to let Dorothy do that she would very much want to do?

Dorothy: Tell me, Sir, Why does the Emerald City need protecting? With the high walls and gatekeepers here, I should think no one would dare to intrude.

Wizard: The Wicked Witch of the West is determined to destroy the Emerald city and all of its citizens. I can never let that happen. Meanwhile you can be sure she will try to make trouble in other ways.

Writer Three: Tell the other ways the Wicked Witch of the West can cause trouble.

Dorothy: Then came that afternoon when the weather went wild.

Writer Four: Describe the wild weather.

Dorothy: I heard a tapping noise on the castle door and when I opened the door there stood the ugliest woman I had ever seen. I wondered how she had gotten past the gatekeepers.

Writer Five: Describe the woman.

Woman: Girl, take me to the Wizard.

Dorothy: I knew this woman was evil. I tried to think of excuses that would make her leave.

Writer Six: Give Dorothy excuses to help get rid of the evil woman.

Dorothy: But the excuses were to no avail. She grabbed my arm and pushed me forward into the Wizard's room.

Wizard: I don't believe it! Not you again! After all these years!

Woman: At last we are face to face, Wizard and now I must give you this.

Dorothy: The woman grabbed the Wizard's hand and put something in it. Then she turned and left the room. When the Wizard opened his hand he was looking at a small piece of paper.

Wizard: No! No! Not that!

Writer Seven: Describe how the shock of what he held affected the Wizard. End our description with his death.

Dorothy: I felt so bad. I had liked the kind Wizard. I began to cry, then through my tears I saw the paper that had fallen from his hand. On one side of the paper was a black spot. On the other side were the words "We are coming after dark." I looked at the wizard's body. His troubles were over but little was I to know that troubles in OZ were just beginning.

Authoring SCARECROW SAVES MUNCHKIN LAND

Reading Parts: Narrator One, Narrator Two, Mayor, Shop Owner, Scarecrow

Narrator One: Long ago the Land of the Munchkins was overrun by blackbirds.

Narrator Two: There were birds on doorsteps and roofs and in gardens.

WRITER ONE: <u>**Tell other places the blackbirds might be.**</u>

Mayor: The blackbird problem is getting worse. This morning my maid was in the garden hanging up the clothes when along came a blackbird and nipped off her nose.

WRITER TWO: <u>**Suggest to the Mayor ways of getting rid of the blackbirds.**</u>

Shop Owner: Wait, here comes the Scarecrow. He knows all about birds. Perhaps he will know what to do.

WRITER THREE: <u>**Describe the Scarecrow.**</u>

Scarecrow: Worry no more, good people. If you have 4 acres to spare where I can build a library, I will get rid of the blackbirds. Every single one. Guaranteed. You see, I want to get a brain, and reading lots of books will help.

Shop Owner: As a member of the Town Council I can assure you that we will give you four acres and help build the library and stock it with all the books you want. Now how are you going to get rid of the blackbirds?

WRITER FOUR: <u>**Pretend the Scarecrow is thinking out loud. What are ways to get rid of the birds?**</u>

Scarecrow: No sooner said than done! Stand back, everyone, the blackbirds will trouble you no more.

Narrator: The Scarecrow lifted his arms and stood still as a statue in the center of town. As the birds flew around him he reached into a sack and threw white powder at each one. As soon as a speck of powder touched their wings, the blackbirds' feathers magically turned to a beautiful snowy white. There were white birds everywhere, swooping down on the citizen's heads and pecking at their noses.

WRITER FIVE: <u>**Tell what the citizens are saying as the birds swoop down on them.**</u>

Scarecrow: Just as I promised, your blackbird problem is solved. Where are the four acres for my library?

Mayor: But you did not get rid of the birds. Look, they are all around us. White birds are just as much of a bother as blackbirds.

Scarecrow: Oh, dear, if I had a brain I could have figured that out.

Narrator One: Feeling quite sad, the Scarecrow began his journey back to the Emerald City. But following behind him were all the birds. They followed him down the street, over the hill and out of the town. For after all, what good is a Scarecrow without birds to scare?

Authoring LITTLE BURNT FACE An Indian Myth

Reading Parts: Narrator, Cruel Sisters, The Great Chief's sister, Little Burnt Face.

NARRATOR:
In a large Algonquin village by a lake lived a poor man with three daughters. He was so poor that

WRITER ONE: Tell how poor the man is. Tell about his food, clothing and wigwam.

NARRATOR:
Two of his daughters were vain and jealous and so cruel to his gentle youngest daughter that they:

WRITER TWO: Tell what mean things the cruel daughters do to the youngest daughter. (Do not include physical violence)

LITTLE BURNT FACE:
Because my sisters are afraid they might get a speck of dirt on their hands, I must tend the fire. The hot coals spit at me like angry snakes and burn and scar my face.

NARRATOR:
Now in the village there also lived a Great Chief and his sister. When a certain spring came, the sister announced that he would marry any girl who could see him.

SISTERS:
There is no doubt that he will choose one of us for we are the most beautiful maidens in the village. We shall dress in our finest garments and go at once to his wigwam.

GREAT CHIEF'S SISTER:
Since you say you can see my brother, tell me what he looks like.

WRITER THREE: What do the cruel sisters say? How do they describe the Great Chief?

GREAT CHIEF'S SISTER:
It's clear that you don't see him at all. You should feel shame at your lies. Be gone with you.

NARRATOR:
Because they were so angry at being turned away, the sisters thought to play a mean trick on Little Burnt Face.

SISTERS: Burnt Face, go at once to the sister of the Great Chief. She has a question you must answer.

NARRATOR:

Poor little Burnt Face! She was a sorry sight.
For her hair was singed off and her face was marked with burns and scars. But she did as she was told and began the walk to the wigwam of the Great Chief.

WRITER FOUR:

Tell what the people say when Burnt Face walks by them on the way to the home of the Great Chief. Tell how they make fun of her appearance.

NARRATOR:

Little Burnt face reached the entrance to the wigwam where the Great Chief was standing beside his sister. But none of the mocking villagers could see him.

SISTER:

Do you see my brother?

BURNT FACE:

I do! I do! And he is wonderful. His sled-string is a beautiful rainbow and his bow-string is the Milky Way.

SISTER:

Yes, you have surely seen him. Come with me to the lake.

WRITER FIVE:

Tell what changes take place in her appearance when Burnt Face bathes in the lake.

NARRATOR:

Then the sister of the Great Chief dressed Burnt Face in a treasured wedding garment and she was most beautiful to behold. .But the two cruel sisters were not invited to the wedding feast. Instead, for the rest of their days they had to

WRITER SIX:

Tell what the mean sisters had to do to get food for themselves and their poor hungry father.

ENTIRE CAST:

And the Great Chief and Little Burnt Face lived happily ever after.

Researching and Authoring PROMETHEUS AND THE GIFT OF FIRE A Greek Myth

Readers: Narrator, Zeus, Prometheus, Hercules, Citizen

NARRATOR: One day Zeus, the King of the Greek gods, looked down on the Kingdom of Man and was not pleased with what he saw.

WRITER ONE: Tell what Zeus saw. What were people doing that displeased Zeus?

ZEUS: I must do something to make man more thankful for the gifts he has been given. I know, I shall take away the gift of fire.

NARRATOR; That is exactly what Zeus did and without fire, man began to suffer greatly.

WRITER TWO: Tell the difficulties and hardships people endured with no fire on Earth.

NARRATOR: Year by year the people of the world became more unhappy. Over and over they asked Zeus to give them back the gift of fire. But Zeus refused.

CITIZEN: We must find a way to get the fire back from Zeus. What can we do?

WRITER THREE: Suggest three ways the people might get the fire back from Zeus.

NARRATOR: All at once a man stood up in the crowd.

PROMETHEUS: I will steal the fire from Zeus. He can see nothing when he sleeps. I will steal it at night. I shall go now!

NARRATOR: Prometheus climbed to the top of Mount Olympus. Without a sound he walked into the room where Zeus slept. He saw the hollow tube in which Zeus kept the fire.

WRITER FOUR: Tell how Prometheus steals the tube of fire. Include a scary moment. Tell the reaction of the people when he brings the fire to them.

NARRATOR: In the morning Zeus found that the hollow tube was gone. He looked down at the Kingdom of Man and saw the people once again using fire.

ZEUS: Messengers of the gods, go down to Earth and find out who has stolen my fire!

NARRATOR: Mercury, his fastest messenger, went to Earth and learned that it was Prometheus who had stolen the fire. Soon Prometheus was standing before Zeus.

PROMETHEUS: I am not afraid. I would steal from you again to help man. It was not right to keep fire from him for so long.

ZEUS: You will never steal from anyone again for I have several proper punishments for you. Let's see. Which one will I choose?

WRITER FIVE: List several punishments. Do not include violent punishment.

ZEUS: Look down, Prometheus. Do you see that far-off rock that overlooks the angry sea. That will be your home for the rest of your days with only a vulture for company.

NARRATOR: So Prometheus was taken to the far off place and for many years lived there chained to the rock. Then one morning he saw a white sail far out at sea. As it came nearer, a powerful man jumped from the boat and swam to the rock.

WRITER SIX: Tell what Prometheus says when he sees the man.

HERCULES: I am Hercules and I have come to save you because you gave the gift of fire back to man. It is my wish to help people who have been kind and good. Come now, let us go back to the world.

PROMETHEUS: Watch out for the vulture which guards me. He will try to kill you.

HERCULES: Let him try! Now let us go.

NARRATOR: Waving his sword, Hercules chased away the ugly bird and with his powerful hands he pulled the chain from the rock. The two swam to the boat and sailed home over the angry sea.

ENTIRE CAST: And Zeus, fearing what Hercules might do next, never bothered Prometheus again.

Researching and Authoring 1776 THE LIBERTY BELL by Nancy Polette

The Liberty Bell rang on July 8, 1776 to summon the citizens of Philadelphia to the first public reading of the Declaration of Independence. In 1996 the bell was once again a cause for rebellion throughout the land. Read on to find out why.

Reading Parts: Narrator, Carlos, Louise, Jenny, Mrs. Evans

NARRATOR: The scene is a sixth grade classroom. The date is April 1, 1996.

LOUISE:　　It is a disgrace! We ought to write the President.

CARLOS:　　Well, somebody should do something. That bell belongs to all the people. How could it be sold? It's a national treasure, even if it did get a crack in it when it was rung in 1776.

JENNY:　　Maybe it was sold by an Act of Congress. Lots of things happen that way. And Carlos, the crack didn't happen in 1776.

WRITER ONE: Tell when the bell was first hung in Independence Hall steeple. What happened to it the first time it was rung?

JENNY:　　Didn't they ever try to fix the crack?

LOUISE:　　I looked it up. It says here that two foundry workers names Pass and Stow melted down the cracked bell and recast it. But when it was rehung in the steeple it rang with a clunk instead of a bong. People covered their ears.

CARLOS:　　Crack or no crack, it still should belong to all the people. The Declaration of Independence says the people have all the power.

WRITER TWO: What is The Declaration of Independence? Who was the man who read it aloud for the first time on July 8, 1776?

LOUISE:　　That's right. And a year later when the British entered Philadelphia it was taken down and hidden so they wouldn't melt it down and use it for cannon.

JENNY:　　Wow, I don't see how they could hide something that big.

WRITER THREE: How much did the Liberty Bell weigh when it was cast?

LOUISE: They hid it in the floorboards in a church in Allentown. That kept the British from getting their hands on it.

CARLOS: But somebody else has their hands on it now and it's not right that one company should own it!

MRS. EVANS: What are you children talking about?

LOUISE: See, it's right here in the New York Times. (Reading from the paper) April 1, 1996.Taco Bell® Buys the Liberty Bell. In an effort to help the national debt, Taco Bell® is pleased to announce that we have agreed to purchase the Liberty Bell, one of our country's most historic treasures. It will now be called the "Taco Liberty Bell" and will still be accessible to the American public for viewing. While some may find this controversial, we hope our move will prompt other corporations to take similar action to do their part to reduce the country's debt.

JENNY: If it's in the paper it must be true.

MRS. EVANS: It is true that newspapers try to be accurate in their stories. What you have overlooked is the most important part of the paper.

NARRATOR: What did the students miss? Do you know?

SUPER RESEARCH CHALLENGE

WRITER FOUR: Find out more about the Taco Liberty Bell. How would anyone reading the full page ad by Taco Bell® know that it was a hoax? Did the hoax increase Taco Bell's® sales?

CO- AUTHOR A TALE OF TERROR WITH RICHARD PECK

The more historical details you can add the more believable your story will be!

Reading Parts: Chip, Computer, Emily

Chip: My name is Chip Chisholm, known at school as Computer Chip. I was just beginning my homework assignment on my word processor when it happened. Miss Beowulf, our English teacher gives assignments you wouldn't believe!

WRITER 1: Describe the "different" kinds of assignments.

Chip: This house we've just moved to is really old, a historic landmark, whatever that is. I guess that's why the lights don't work. Look at the way my computer screen keeps flashing on and off. But wait . . . is that a message?

Computer: To the boy in the attic . . . I have been waiting for you many years. You will find me underneath the cellar floor . . . I am but bones now but once I lived. Come find me in my prison, learn my secret and set me free . . . There will be a reward, naturally.

Chip: Seeing that, you can bet I made my way down the stairs. The cellar was really dark. It has a brick floor. Some of the things down there look like they could have been there for 100 years.

WRITER 2: Name the items Chip sees. Be sure to include some unusual ones.

Chip: I dropped to my knees. I reached for a brick and when I touched it, it was as warm as . . . life. A cyclone of dust blinded me . . . then I heard in a shriek of sound . . . words!

Emily: At . . . last. Free . . . at . . . last!

Chip: I couldn't believe what I saw. She was standing there before me looking just the way she might have looked 100 years ago.

WRITER 3: <u>Describe the girl and her gown. Be as authentic as possible.</u>

Emily: How long I have waited. Ages and ages. And how painful my death, here among strangers.

Chip: Your death? Are you dead?

Emily: Oh, quite. And I shouldn't have died at all. After all, I was only visiting!

WRITER 4: <u>Describe how Emily died in an actual disaster that happened in the 1800s or very early 1900s. Be sure to explain how she came to be buried under the floor.</u>

Emily: It's a sad thing to be left in an unmarked grave so far from my real home.

Chip: You're not happy here?

Emily: Who would be? I want to go home!

Chip: And if I don't find some way to help you, you'll be haunting this house and me on a permanent basis? Oh, wow, what can I do?

Emily: I know you will think of something. There has to be a way to get my bones back where they belong.

WRITER 5: <u>Give Chip a way to return the bones to their final resting place.</u>

Emily: I just knew these folks would be full of ideas . . . don't you think? Which one will you choose, Chip?

Chip: I like <u>(chooses one idea)</u>

Emily: I promised you a reward. The next time you turn on your strange machine you'll see it right there in bright words.

Chip: She was right. And the reward was something I've always wanted and sure could use . . . it was . . .

WRITER 6: <u>Tell what the reward was.</u>

TRANSFORMING NARRATIVE TO DIALOGUE

It is possible to create readers theatre scripts from any form of narrative...a book jacket blurb, an Aesop's Fable, a paragraph from the science or social studies text are good examples. There is no expense involved, no props or costumes are used, and the readers theatre group both prepares and performs its own script.

PREPARING THE SCRIPT

Students in the upper primary grades through high school can quickly be taught to turn any piece of narrative writing into a readers theatre script. The procedure is as follows:

1. Read the piece together with each person reading a line in turn.
2. Decide on the characters who will speak.
3. Decide on which characters will need narrators.
4. Narrator speaking parts can be marked N1 for narrator one and N2 for narrator two. Each narrator reads those lines which apply to his or her character.
5. Words which indicate what a character is thinking, feeling or doing can be spoken by that character. Characters' parts can be indicated with the first letter or letters of the characters' names.
6. NO WORDS IN THE SELECTION ARE CHANGED. The integrity of the text must be kept.

Study the sample booktalk that follows to see how it is turned into a readers theatre. script.
The Righteous Revenge of Artemis Bonner by Walter Dean Myers. HarperCollins, 1992
N1 = Narrator One; N2 = Narrator Two; A = Artemis; C = Catfish

N1
In 1880 two important events took place. | N2 Catfish Grimes | C shot dead Ugly Ned Bonner, |
N2 Uncle to Artemis Bonner and | N1 A Artemis headed west to avenge Uncle Ugly's death and
N1 find the gold mine | left to him in his Uncle's will. | N2 Catfish Grimes | C is determined not to
N2 be caught. | He would also like | C to find the gold mine before Artemis does. | N1 But Artemis
A has the strength | of TRUE DETERMINATION! | N1 He tracks Catfish | A from Mexico to Alaska
N2 and back again. | Finally they meet in a shootout | N1 in front of the Bird Cage Saloon. |
N2 Catfish yelled, | C "When I count three, go for your gun." | N2 No sooner had he shouted
C "One!" | N1 than both Catfish and Artemis drew. | N2 Read <u>The Righteous Revenge of Artemis</u>
N1 Bonner | to discover the exciting finish to this romp through the Old West.

SAMPLE SCRIPT: <u>The Righteous Revenge of Artemis Bonner</u> by Walter Dean Myers. HarperCollins, 1992.

Here is the same jacket copy from the previous page in script form. Additional phrases (in italics) have been added to make the play livelier.

Speaking Parts: N1=Narrator One, N2=Narrator Two, A=Artemis, C=Catfish

Narrator 1:	In 1880 two important events took place.
Narrator 2:	Catfish Grimes
Catfish:	Shot dead Ugly Ned Bonner. POW! POW! TAKE THAT, AND THAT, AND THAT!
Narrator 2:	Uncle to Artemis Bonner and
Narrator 1:	Artemis
Artemis:	headed west to avenge Uncle Ugly's death and find the gold mine (you bet!)
Narrator 1:	left to him in his Uncle's will.
Narrator 2:	Catfish Grimes
Catfish:	is determined not to be caught. NO JAIL TIME FOR ME!
Narrator 2:	He would also like
Catfish:	to find the gold mine before Artemis does.
Narrator 1:	But Artemis has the strength
Artemis:	of TRUE DETERMINATION. (That means I don't give up.)
Narrator 1:	He tracks Catfish
Artemis:	from Mexico to Alaska and back again. (I'll need a new pair of boots if this keeps up.)
Narrator 2:	Finally they meet in a shootout
Narrator 1:	in front of the Bird Cage Saloon.
Narrator 2:	Catfish yelled
Catfish:	When I count three go for your gun. (That kid is so dumb he won't know what hit him.)
Narrator 2:	No sooner had he shouted
Catfish:	ONE!
Narrator 1:	Than both Catfish and Artemis drew.
Catfish & Artemis:	(POW, POW, BANG, BANG POW POW, BANG BANG POW!)
Narrator 2:	Read The Righteous Revenge of Artemis Bonner
Narrator 1:	to discover the exciting finish to this romp through the Old West.
Entire Cast:	(GO WEST, YOUNG MAN, GO WEST. YOU WON'T BE SORRY!)

FOR PRACTICE

Follow the example given for <u>The Righteous Revenge of Artemis Bonner</u> and mark these jacket blurbs to turn them into readers theatre scripts.

George Washington's Mother by Jean Fritz. Putnam, 1993.

George Washington's mother did not like fancy parties, teas or dressing up. She worried about two things: Being poor, and son, George, who was always ready for a fight and every time an army was put together, he joined it! When he returned to Mount Vernon after each battle his mother would beg him not to leave again. Trouble grew in the Colonies. George heard that the King of England was sending an army to control the Colonists. He knew that the colonies needed an army, too, and someone to lead it. Would George stay home as his mother wished? Just ask George Washington's mother.

This Time Tempe Wick by Patricia Lee Gauch. Putnams, 1974.

In the winter of 1779 more than 10,000 troops settled in Jockey Hollow around the farm where Tempe Wick lived. To help the soldiers, Tempe Wick shared food and clothing and even mended shattered uniforms. The soldiers were hungry and cold and hadn't been paid when they stormed across the Wick farm, shooting off a cannon and shouting "We Quit!" Tempe brought her horse Bonnie into the house, picked up a rifle and barred the door. Give us your horse the soldiers demanded, and that was when Tempe Wick got storming, had quite enough mad! What happened next was as surprising to the soldiers as it was to the usually even-tempered Tempe Wick.

Activity Mark these jacket blurbs to turn them into readers theatre scripts.

THE BITE OF THE GOLD BUG: THE ALASKAN GOLD RUSH by Barthe DeClements. Viking, 1992.

"There's thousands of dollars in gold just waiting for us," Uncle Tanner told Buck's family. "Just stake me to the trip and we'll go and get it, and this time I promise not to gamble it away." Uncle Tanner had just arrived from the Alaskan gold fields and Bucky could feel the excitement of gold just for the taking. So Bucky and Pa and Uncle Tanner do head for Alaska, facing stormy oceans and long trails with heavy packs and climbs of fifteen hundred feet straight up a mountainside. The three make it to the claim site and work for months to separate tiny flecks of gold from the mud and gravel. Then Uncle Tanner volunteers to take the gold to Dawson City to have it weighed. When he doesn't return, Bucky begins to wonder if THE BITE OF THE GOLD BUG has become the bite of the gambling bug. Has it all been for nothing?

THE GHOSTS OF WAR by Daniel Cohen. Putnam's, 1990.

On August 12, 1812 Lt. William Muir was killed in a battle between the British and the Americans. The night before the battle he visited his sweetheart and begged her to pledge her love forever. Playing hard-to-get, the girl, Marie, told William that there might be other young men she liked better, although she knew that William was the one she truly loved. That same night Marie was awakened by the sound of footsteps and saw the ghostly figure of William with ghastly wounds. The figure reached out to touch her and spoke softly to her. In the morning Marie remembered the words and looked at her hand. She cried out at what she saw, knowing without a doubt that she had been visited by one of the GHOSTS OF WAR.

AS FAR AS MILL SPRINGS by Patricia Pendergraft. Philomel, 1992.

The cold winter and the Depression have hit hard, and like most of the orphans at the Hixon's, Robert has lived in one foster home or another for most of his life. But one day, just before Christmas, old man Hixon punishes Robert with such cruelty that the boy runs away determined to find his real mother and his own home. Robert, however, has not gone far when he finds he has not run away alone. His friend, the young Abiah, follows him. "I'd rather die than stay in that place another minute," she tells Robert. Then they meet up with Mutt dog and together they head off for Mill springs, riding the rails and braving cold and hunger as they go. Then in a race to jump a fast moving train, Robert and Abiah are separated. Will they ever meet again? Is a family waiting in Mill Springs for either of the children?

LITERATURE AND

THE SOCIAL STUDIES

Almost any picture book or junior novel can be used to teach or review social studies concepts. Human rights are explored in the powerful novel. <u>The Giver</u>. An entire course in economics could be taught with Jean Merrill's <u>Pushcart War</u>. War and its consequences are starkly portrayed in the picture books <u>Hiroshima No Pika</u> and <u>The Cello of Mr. O</u>. Titles too numerous to list deal with all phases of American history.

A closer look at almost any literature will reveal a wide variety of social studies concepts. <u>The Wonderful Wizard of Oz</u> by L. Frank Baum is a good example.

A. Concept Understand how people's positions and experiences influence their views of events by (a) expressing the point of view of the Munchkins vs the Witch of the West at the death of the Witch of the East (b) find other differences in points of view in the story.

B. Concept Understand the rights and responsibilities of citizens in democratic societies by citing the many ways Dorothy & companions worked together to achieve their goal.

C. Concept: Understand the processes by which citizens can resolve disputes by examining the long standing dispute of the Wizard and the Wicked Witch of the West and suggesting ways in which it might have been peacefully resolved.

D. Concept Understand that all decisions have consequences by examining the varied decisions of the characters: For example, "What was the consequence of Dorothy going to find Toto instead of going to the storm cellar when Aunt Em called?" "What other situations in the book dealt with decisions and their consequences?"

E. Concept Understand cause/effect relationships related to the behavior of individuals and groups by discussing the following:
    Because Dorothy's house landed on the witch . . .
    Because the Tin Man's joints were rusted . . .
    Because the Scarecrow was made of straw . . .
    Because the Wizard was not a real wizard . . .

F. Concept Understand the variations among cultures by examining the lifestyles of: The Munchkins, The people of the Emerald City, The Hammerheads, The China People, The people of the Kingdom of The Wicked Witch of the West.

The above concepts are but a few of those that apply to people and nations and can be easily introduced as the literature is shared. Look at children's literature with a third eye, one seeking deeper themes and concepts that can be shared and the literature will become an integral part of every social studies program, bringing the past alive and developing a greater understanding of the individual's relationship to his or her world and the human beings that inhabit it.

TEACHING THINKING SKILLS FOR SOCIAL STUDIES

1. ANALYZE

A. Read the material!

B. Break down the material to basic parts.

C. Discover the relationship between ideas

D. Develop a list of related facts about each part.

Example   Select categories to use in comparing inventors. Were any two or more alike in any way?

NAME	EARLY LIFE	FATHER'S PROFESSION	INVENTOR'S PROFESSION	AGE ACHIEVED FAME
Fulton	made unique items for mom	farmer	artist	30
Bell	experimented with sound	teacher	teacher	28
Whitney	made a violin at age 12	farmer	teacher	28
Edison	worked with chemicals at 9	manufacturer	telegrapher	32
Morse	worked with electricity	businessman	artist	46
Wright	made toys	minister	printer	32

2. GENERALIZE (Use the chart above)

A. Collect, organize and examine data.

B. Identify common elements or what is generally true.

C. State a generalization based on common elements.

D. Check against data to see if it holds up.

Example Collect information about more inventors. Compare with the information given in the chart. Does the generalization hold up? What generally can be said about the author's books or writings?

3. SYNTHESIZE

A. Clarify the purpose of what is to be produced.

B. Identify the basic parts or items to be used.

C. Identify the form(s) of presentation.

D. Plan and proceed with synthesis.

Example Combine five or more of the items below to invent a bedroom burglar alarm. One item will act on the next which will act on the next and so on until the alarm goes off: cat, ice cubes, match book, cuckoo clock, pigeon, cannon, horn, metal spring, bucket, saw, tea kettle, balloon, 50 pound weight, candle, frog, magnet, umbrella.

4. PROBLEM SOLVING/DECISION MAKING.

A. Define the problem.

B. List possible solutions or alternatives.

C. Establish criteria for rating choices.

D. Rate each alternative 1=no, 2=maybe 3=yes

E. The alternative with the highest total is the one to choose.

Example Suppose you could time trek back to 1776 and found yourself in Colonial Boston with nothing but the clothes you are wearing. What could you share with the Colonists that would improve their lives?

IDEAS	Will help many	Able to share	Will be accepted	Total

5. EVALUATION

A. Identify what is to be evaluated.

B. Define standards of appraisal.

C. Collect data related to defined standards.

D. Apply data and make a judgement.

Example

A. List five well-known characters from literature.

B. List the qualities of a good leader (defining standards for judgement)

C. Which of these characters best meets the standards listed in B?

What do you know about the leadership abilities of each character?

D. Apply data and make a judgement.

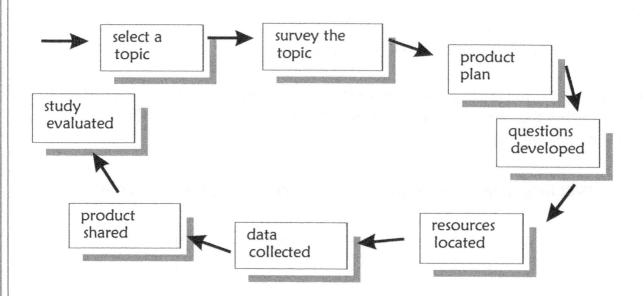

Select a topic and **survey the topic** to determine what you know about it and what you would like to find out.

Develop a **product plan** or task to be accomplished. **Example** I will write a Fact and Fiction Book about Abraham Lincoln which details his struggles, achievements and influence on others in North America and throughout the world.

Develop Questions: What were Lincoln's major accomplishments? What struggles did he have to contend with? How did his accomplishments have an impact on the United States? . . . on the world?

Determine Resources: List specific books, magazine articles, Internet sites.

Collect and Organize Data: Gather data to answer the questions and arrange or organize as a Fact and Fiction Book. Make a statement about Lincoln on one page. On the next page tell your reader the statement is fact or fiction and why.
The book should be a minimum of twelve pages.

Share the Product with others.

Evaluate: Does the Fact and Fiction Book contain all needed information? Could any part of the research process be done more efficiently?

INTERESTING FORMATS FOR REPORTING INFORMATION

ABC Sequence

Gathering the Sun by Alma Flor Ada. William Morrow. 1997.
Hispanic culture from A-Z told in Spanish and English.
A is for arboles (trees) **C** is for Caesar Chavez
A Is for Africa by I. Onyefulu. Viking, 1993.
A Is for Asia by C. Chinn-Lee. Orchard, 1999.

Time Sequence

The Boston Tea Party by Pamela Edwards. Putnam, 2001 (House That Jack Built format)
"These are the leaves that grew on a bush in a far off land that became part of the Boston Tea Party. This is the tea that was made from the leaves . . .
Example using the format
This is the paper made from the trees that grew in the woods that became part of the Constitution.
These are the colonists who demanded self government who wrote on the paper made from the trees that grew in the woods that became part of the Constitution.
These are the rights guaranteed to all citizens written by the colonists on the paper made from the trees that grew in the woods that became part of the Constitution.

Sir Frances Drake, His Daring Deeds by Roy Gerrard. Farrar, 1988. (Sequential events in poetry form).
> "When Frances Drake was only ten he went to sea with grown-up men
> And flabbergasted all the crew by quickly learning what to do."

Example using the format:

In Canada this babe was born
Early on a summer morn
Played with toys and played with blocks
His parents named him Michael Fox.

Went to school and hit the books
Girls were awed by his good looks
Thought that he might televise
In the cast of Family Ties.

While his part was pretty groovy
Decided he would make a movie
Played the part, Doc Hollywood
Fans thought he was pretty good.

While life's blows are most ironic
Brought down by disease most chronic
Parkinson's in middle age
Took this actor from the stage.

He's determined, he is sure
Someday there will be a cure.
He won't quit, despite the shocks
For his name is Michael Fox.

Iron Horses by Verla Kay. Putnam, 2000.
The story of the building of the transcontinental railroad from the initial idea to completion.
Told in rapid poetry form.
> "Railroad barons, visions, dreams, thinking, planning, plotting schemes.
> Politicians, Congress, Vote. 'Build your railroad,' Lincoln wrote."

Example using the format. Relating a historical event in poetry form.

How Tad Lincoln Saved Jack,	Interrupted
the White House Turkey,	The President
For Thanksgiving	Please, Sir
Holiday	I don't want
Big fat turkey	him killed
Came to stay	President
White House	Nodded
Dinner	Voice was stilled.
Table Set	Stop the
Cooking up	Pleading
Tads	Do not
Turkey pet	Grieve
Tad refused	Here's a
Its life	President's
To end	Reprieve.
For the	Turkey's life
Turkey was	Was to be
his friend.	Spared.
Into Chambers	Lincoln showed
Young Tad	He really
went	Cared.

Compare and Contrast
So You Want to Be President? by Judith St. George. Philomel, 2000.

Compares presidents by names. childhood, physical appearance, personalities, siblings, children, pets, musical or artistic ability, level of education, favorite pastimes, jobs.

Activity   Select any occupational group: astronauts, inventors, world leaders, or other category. Research the lives of six to eight people in the group and compare using the categories found in So You Want To Be President?

Christmas In The Big House, Christmas In The Quarters by Pat and Fred McKissack.
Scholastic, 1994.
Pattern:
If I lived in _____
I would _____ (List 4-6 Christmas events)
But I wouldn't (list 4-6 events that take place in another locale)
because _____ did that.

© 2003 Nancy Polette

<u>**Example**</u> using the format
 If I lived in the Big House
 I would find many presents under the tree
 And sing by the Yule Log
 And east roast turkey with trimmings
 And go to sleep under a down comforter.
 But I wouldn't wake up to no tree and no gifts
 And sing sad songs
 And eat fat and greens
 And sleep on a sack on the floor
 Because slaves in the Quarters did that.

Cause and Effect

<u>Accidents May Happen: Fifty Inventions Discovered by Mistake</u> by Charlotte Foltz.
HarperCollins, 1998.
<u>Earthquakes</u> by Seymour Simon. Mulberry, 1995.
Write about an important event during the school year. What was the reason for the event
(cause), what happened (effect)? Bind copies and give to the local historical society.

Show Problems and Solutions

<u>Trouble at the Mines</u> by Doreen Rappaport. Harper, 1998.
The mine workers had been on strike so long that they decided to go back to work so their
children wouldn't starve. Going back to work, however, meant they would continue to
subsist on starvation wages. See how the problem is solved when Mary Harris Jones arrives
on the scene.

<u>Forging Freedom</u> by Hudson Talbot. Putnam, 2001.
A Dutch printer sees many of his Jewish friends taken to concentration camps. They need
papers to protect them, but authentic copies of the needed documents can only be obtained
from the Nazi headquarters in Paris. How will Jaap Penrat solve the problem?

<u>Mary On Horseback</u> by Rosemary Wells. Dial, 2000.
In the 1930s the people of Appalachia had no medical care. Many homes were inaccessible
except by horseback. Mary Breckenridge solved the problem by starting the Frontier
Nursing Service where medical help was brought to isolated areas by horseback.

Social History in Song

Many musicians and singers have turned to song as a means of recording social history. The
beautiful illustrated picture book <u>From A Distance</u> by Julie Gold, Dutton, 2000 shows the
contrasts of life in peace and war and is especially powerful if shared with the Bette Midler
recording.

Woody Guthrie was a folklorist historian who recorded social history as he lived it.

Read: <u>Woody Guthrie, Poet of the People</u> by Bonnie Christensen. Knopf, 2001.
This book celebrates the times and the spirit of folk musician, Woody Guthrie. His most
famous song, "This Land Is Your Land," is sung today nearly as often as the national
anthem. And his songs expressing the thoughts and feelings of ordinary Americans during
the Great Depression and the 1940s are still heard wherever people gather to sing out for
peace or the environment or justice.

Activity

Research a problem in your community. Write words to the tune of "This Land Is Your Land" to help citizens become aware of the problem.

A report on a clean-up site where uranium waste has seeped into ground water is sung to the tune of "This Land Is Your Land."

It was in Weldon Springs
That they made uranium
For the bombs of World War Two
Now the plant sits empty
But radioactive waste
Seeps in the ground water
This land destroyed for you and me.

No one will clean it up
Say it's too costly
But a school sits nearby
And the cancer rate's soaring
It was in Weldon Springs
They made uranium
This land destroyed for you and me.

WHAT MAKES A GOOD BIOGRAPHY?

1. It has a beginning that "hooks" the reader.

"Hurry, children. You can't be late"!
"I want to go home," little Wolfgang Mozart told his father.
"You can't go home," his father said. "You must play for the king."

2. It tells WHEN and WHERE.
Wolfgang was tired. By 1762 he had played for Kings and Queens all over Europe. He was only six years old.

3. It is filled with action, revealing the character by WHAT the person does. Wolfgang did not have time for games like other children. He spent hours and hours practicing the harpsichord and writing new music.

4. It reveals the person by what others say.
"He is the wonder boy of the age," the people said. "Imagine a child writing an opera for the Emperor of Austria!"

5. It shows difficulties that were overcome.
Wolfgang's dream when he grew up was to be a composer for a court. Instead, he had to work for a strict and unkind man. But this did not stop him from writing more music.

6. It tells of the person's accomplishments.
Before he died at age 35 Wolfgang Mozart had written twenty operas and 41 symphonies. His music is often played today. Wouldn't you like to hear it?

Play: "The Mozart Effect. Music for Children" Volume 1 Track One (Rondo) The Children's Group, Inc. 1997 Atlantic Recording Corp.

Check out these easy-to-read biographies. Do they have all the elements above?

Bessie Coleman Queen of the Sky by Linda Johns. Illustrated by Stephen Harrington. Wright Group, 2000.
Bessie Coleman, the first black woman aviator, proved that nothing could stop her from reaching high places. She showed young people everywhere that dreams of flight can come true.

Oseola McCarty Woke Up the World by Barbara Diamond. Illustrated by Dan Brown. Wright Group, 2001.
After working hard all her life, when she was 86 years old, Oseola McCarty gave $280,000 to the University of Mississippi to help young people get an education.

WRITING A BIOGRAPHY

1. Find 3-5 items of information to place under each heading in the data bank.
2. Follow instructions below for the kinds of sentences to include in the biography. Include the information from the data bank.
3. Proofread your report for correct spelling and sentence structure.
4. List the source(s) of your information.

Kate Shelley Data Bank

Lived
Iowa - 1881
Near Honey Creek
By train tracks
On a farm
Near Des Moines River
Clapboard house

Description
15 years old
dark hair
work-worn hands
brave
responsible
hard working

What She Did
plowed and planted
ran the family farm
shot hawks
rode bareback
read a lot
prevented a train wreck

Related To
deceased father (railroad man)
invalid mother
sister Mayme, brother John
deceased brother James

Remembered For
making dangerous journey
alone at night in a storm to stop trains from
    crossing a bridge that was out

A REPORT ABOUT KATE SHELLEY

Write an eight sentence biography report that:

1. Has a beginning question that involves the reader.

2. Tells who, what, when, where.

3. Includes action words that tell what is happening.

4. Shows cause and effect.

5. Shows difficulties that were overcome.

6. Tells what others say about the person.

7. Tells of the person's accomplishments

8. Has a concluding sentence that uses a universal word (we, all of us, everyone, everywhere, everybody, always, nobody, every time, every day)

Source: Kate Shelley: Bound for Legend by Robert San Souci. Dial, 1995.

TEACHING ECONOMICS

The Pushcart War by Jean Merrill. Harper & Row, 1964.

FIND SOMEONE . . . (A name can be used only once)
1. Who did a good job because a reward was promised. _____
(incentive/reward)
2. Has spent money to make money._____ (venture capital)
3. Has paid a high price for something because it was scarce. _____
(supply & demand)
4. Has paid someone for advice. _____(investment in human resources)
5. Can name a company that is the only supplier of goods or services in your community.
_____ (monopoly)
6. Who sold cookies as well as lemonade at a lemonade stand. _____
(diversification)
7. Has found a fast way to make a lot of something. _____ (mass production)
8. Has seen gas stations compete by dropping prices. _____ (price war)
9. Has taken something to sell with the understanding that unsold items can be returned.
_____ (consignment)
10. Has watched TV instead of doing homework even though unfinished homework means
problems at school. _____ (opportunity cost)

Find examples of the economic terms above in the booktalk that follows.

"If It's A Big Job, Why Not Make It A MAMMOTH Job?" Advertising was one of the
reasons the Mammoth Trucking Company had taken over the streets of New York. Because
the trucks were so big and the pushcarts were so small, when the two met, guess who got
the worst of it? Maxie Hammerman, the only pushcart repair man in New York, was kept
extra busy these days. The Pushcart vendors called a meeting to make plans to stop the
trucks from damaging the carts. Frank the Flower was there (he always gave his customers
13 flowers when they paid for 12, bringing down the price among the other flower sellers).
Harry the Hot Dog sold food but was thinking of adding other items to his cart. General
Anna sold apples. She picked them up at the market early in the morning and could return
at the end of the day any she did not sell. "Well," Harry the Hot Dog argued, "If we take
time away to fight the trucks, we will have to take time away from selling. I might lose
customers." "Believe me," said General Anna, "If we don't fight we won't have a business
left."
Problem: How can the pushcart vendors stay in business?
List your solutions on the grid below. Rate each idea 1=no 2=maybe 3=yes

Ideas	Fast	Safe	Low cost	Effective	Total

REPORTING ON A STATE, COUNTRY OR PROVINCE

1. A Song
She'll be coming from (CAPITAL) when she comes.
She'll be coming from (LARGE CITY) when she comes
She'll bring (THREE PRODUCTS)
She'll bring (THREE CROPS)
She'll be coming from (COUNTRY, STATE OR PROVINCE) when she comes.

2. A Pattern
If I visited the (COUNTRY, STATE, PROVINCE) of _____
I could (list six to eight things you could see or do there.
But I couldn't (name one sight or activity you could do in another country, state or province
Because I'd do or see that in _____.

3. Fortunately Report
Choose a famous person from the country, state or province you are writing about. In chronological order, list five positive and five negative things that happened in the person's life. All facts must be well researched to show the source of each.
   Example A Famous Person from Virginia
      Fortunately Robert E. Lee was appointed Superintendent of West Point.
      Unfortunately he preferred to be in the field.
      Fortunately he had a great devotion for his family and friends.
      Unfortunately he was asked by the president to lead armies to fight against them.

4. The Mystery Country, State or Province Report
List ten clues or facts about the country, state or province. Ask a classmate to give a number between one and ten. One clue must be the capital. Read the clue for that number. The student can guess or pass. The game continues until the country, state or province is guessed or all clues are read.

5. The Letter pattern. Use the first letter of the country, state or province name and complete the pattern.
   Example for Texas
      T my name is Teresa
      My husband's name is Tom
      We come from Texas
      And we sell Tortillas, Tamales and Ten gallon hats. (Three crops or products)
      Teresa is a tarantula (native animal)
      Tom is a turkey. (native animal)

6. Food
The (king, president, prime minister) is coming to dinner. Prepare a menu that uses only foods raised or grown in the place you are writing about. All ingredients must come from that place as well.

INTRODUCING ANCIENT EGYPT WITH LITERATURE

1. SHARE THE EGYPTIAN CINDERELLA by Shirley Climo. Harper, 1989.

In the Land of Egypt where the green Nile River widens to meet the blue sea, lives a maiden called Rhodopes. Because she is Greek and a slave, she is scorned by the other house servants. She has only her rose-red slippers which flash like fireflies when she dances. When a falcon swoops down and snatches a slipper away, Rhodopes is heartbroken. How is she to know that the falcon has delivered the slipper to the great Pharaoh himself? She cannot guess that the Pharaoh will search all of Egypt to find the owner of the tiny shoe and make her his queen.

DEBATE The Pharaoh was considered not only a ruler but a god and could have many wives. If a wife displeased him he could have her killed. Debate: Should Rhodopes marry the Pharaoh?

Before debating read about the Pharaoh and his wives in: The Awesome Egyptians by Terry Deary and Peter Hepplewhite. Scholastic, 1997.

2. Share the book and excerpts from the opera. AIDA told by Leontyne Price. Illustrated by Leo and Diane Dillon. Harcourt Brace, 1990. Adapted from the opera by Giuseppe Verdi.

Aida is a royal princess of the African nation of Ethiopia. The proud and beautiful girl loved her father and her country above all else. When she is captured by Egyptian soldiers, she is made a slave to the daughter of the Pharaoh, Amneris. Aida hides her true identity and serves her new mistress well until she and Radames, a captain in the Egyptian army fall in love. Amneris also loves the captain and her jealousy leads her to betray him. Radames is sentenced to death as a traitor and Aida must choose between loyalty to her country or death with her true love.

Sing OPERA KARAOKE from Aida
at: http://www.opera.it/English/Opere/Aida/Curiosit.html

3. SHARE A Place in the Sun by Jill Rubalcaba. Viking PRess. 1998.
Senmet is sentenced to a life of slavery for accidentally killing a dove. Here is an exciting story that reveals life in ancient Egypt.

4. ABOUT THE PYRAMIDS
Answer these questions. Guess if you do not know.
Support or deny your answers by checking the data bank on the next page.
1. The base of the Great Pyramid of Cheops is a square with each side being

_____ feet in length.
2. The burial chamber inside the Great Pyramid was_____feet high.
3. It took _____men _____years to finish a pyramid.
4. The Great Pyramid is made of _____stone blocks.
5. There are _____known pyramids in Egypt.
Total your answers_____

A PYRAMID DATA BANK
(The Great Pyramid)

LOCATION
Egypt
West bank of Nile
In the desert

DESCRIPTION
754ft X 754ft
2,300,000 stone blocks
16 million cubic feet
Hidden passages & trapdoors

CONTENTS
Tomb for Pharaoh
Pharoah's treasures
Religious writings
Servants and pets

USES
Stone computer
Observatory
Burial place
Giant calendar
Sundial

OTHER FACTS
Took 80,000 men five years to build the Great Pyramid
Most robbed of treasures within 200 years of completion
Mummies sometimes buried with model dolls
Went out of fashion between 1800 BC and 800BC
96 pyramids in Egypt

5. PUTTING HISTORY BACK TOGETHER

These bits of history, if put in the correct order, will tell you the sad tale of a young queen. Who was she? What happened to her first husband? Who did she marry after her husband's death?

_____

Birth Announcement:

Mr. & Mrs. Ay are proud new grandparents of a baby girl named Ankhesenamum (Ank for short)

_____

Uncle Ay's Journal Entry: Tut will never guess the enormous power I now have!

_____

News Headline: Nine-year-old King Tut assumes throne. Uncle to act as advisor.

_____

News Headline: Mysterious Death of 18-year-old Tut

_____

Marriage Announcement: 17-year-old Tut marries Ankhesenamum and makes her his queen.

_____

Conversation between Tut and Wife: It is time I began to rule Egypt. Uncle Ay must go.

_____

Death Notice: Mrs. Ay dies.

_____

Marriage Announcement: Ay, advisor to deceased King Tut, marries King's widow and becomes the new king.

_____

Susanna of the Alamo by John Jakes. Harcourt, 1986.

Before dawn on Sunday March 6, Santa Anna's armies were stirring. Dozing in an old damp blanket with Angelina in her arms, Susanna woke suddenly. "What is that music?" she whispered. Guns were crackling outside the chapel. Artillery matches glowed near the cannon on the walls. Susanna stared into the horrified face of her friend, Senora Espanza. "Santa Anna is tormenting us," the Senora replied. "The music means, 'Show No Mercy! Kill Everyone!' Sharp as knives the bugle notes flew through the air. Susanna clutched her baby. She heard shouting and ladders thumping against the Alamo walls. Susanna's heart beat fast. She looked at the women. All the faces shared the same look. They seemed to say, 'We are frightened but we stayed here to show what we were made of. Now it is time.' "

1. Pre Reading Activity Work with a partner to answer these questions. Guess if you do not know. Then read Susanna of the Alamo to support or deny your guesses.
  A. How many men defended the Alamo? _____
  B. How old was their leader, Col. Travis? _____
  C. How wide (in yards) was the gap between the south wall and the chapel? _____
  D. How many volunteers did Davy Crockett bring with him? _____
  E. How old was Davy Crockett when he died at the Alamo? _____
  F. Santa Anna's army could not have been less than ____ men.

2. Vocabulary Activity
  HAVE A SENTENCE CONTEST: Working with a partner or a group of three, make a sentence using as many of these words as possible. You may add other words as needed.
  _____ adobe   _____ Goliad   _____ Travis   _____ los alamos
  _____ grenadiers _____ Zapadores   _____ Gonzalez   _____ palisade
  _____ cavalry   _____ sacristy   _____ artillery   _____ mission
  _____ siege   _____ Santa Anna _____ norteamericanos

3. Pre Reading Journal Sentence Starters
Choose one of the sentence starters that follow. Finish the sentence and continue to write on the topic for five minutes. Be prepared to share what you have written with others.
A. Settling in an unfamiliar land would be . . .
B. Strength can be shown in many ways . . .
C. Freedom is worth defending because . . .
D. Revenge can never be rewarding because . . .

Key for #1: A. 182 B. 27 C. 17 D. 12 E. 50 F. 4000

4. Point of View (Authors)
Have one student take the role of Travis and explain why freedom from Mexico is important. Have the SAME student take the role of Santa Anna and explain why the rebels in Texas should be subdued.

LOCATION
Texas
Center of San Antonio

DESCRIPTION
Spanish mission, architecture
high walls
small
surrounded by cottonwood trees

PURPOSE
Built as a mission 1718
Monastery, church
Religion
Protection
Texans used as a fort

THE ALAMO
DATA BANK

EVENTS
Feb./Mar. 1836
182 Texans held off Santa Anna's
army of 4-6 thousand for 13 days
Texans ran out of ammunition
Overwhelmed by Mexican army
All Texans killed except for
women and children

PEOPLE INVOLVED
Lt. Col. William Travis
Jim Bowie
Davy Crockett
Santa Anna

OTHER FACTS
Allowed Sam Houston
time to build an army
to save the independence
movement of Texas

Label notes: **L** = location **D**=description **P**=purpose **E**=events **PE**=people **O**=other facts
When writing the report keep all items together which have the same label.

Labels	Main Ideas	Why?	Compare/Contrast
P	Built as mission 1718	for religious meetings	church
D	Made of stone, wood	only materials available	other buildings in area
D	High walls	protection	fort
E	1836 Santa Anna's army	to keep Texas for Mexico	
E	182 Texans vs 4-6000 Mexicans		few Greeks vs. many Persians at Thermopylac
E	Texans held out 13 days	to give S. Houston time to gather an army	
E	All Texas fighters killed	Santa Anna vowed to "give no quarter"	
D	Surrounded by cotton-wood trees	shade from sun	
PE	Jim Bowie, Davy Crockett fought	wanted freedom for Texans	like Col. Travis
E	Women and children spared	Santa Anna wanted to show humanity	
PE	Susanna Dickinson and baby freed	to tell of Santa Anna kindness	slaves freed
L	Center San Antonio, TX	accessible to all	City Hall

THE INDUCTIVE REASONING BOOK REPORT

In visiting their Aunt on Staten Island, two sisters want to find out who the strange woman was who died in the house next door well over 100 years earlier. It seems that the local people believe there is a ghost that haunts the house . . . the ghost of the mysterious young woman who, the tale goes, was dropped off at the house on a stormy night in the 1860s when she became ill. The woman had a small child with her. The woman died and the child was raised by the kindly couple who owned the house. They never found out who she was. You, however, can solve the mystery by sharing the clues in the four boxes!

1. Who was the strange woman?
2. What do the words "butcher" and "alma" mean?
3. Why was the woman traveling?

CLUE CARD ONE

In 1989 the old Bennett house is haunted by a stagecoach that pulls up to the front door on rainy nights.

In the 1860s a stagecoach ran from Richmond Town to Watering Place where passengers could take a ferry to New York.

In 1855 General Santa Anna escaped by sea after his overthrow as Emperor of Mexico. Gilbert Thompson and Clyde Dibney smuggled Santa Anna out of Richmond Town in an old piano box. The schooner carrying the piano box was wrecked but Santa Anna was one of the few to live through the wreck.

READ: <u>Mystery of the Strange Traveler</u> by Phyllis Whitney, MacMillan, 1951.

CLUE CARD TWO

On a rainy night in 1864 a stagecoach pulled up to the Bennett House.

The young woman died and her child Serena, was raised by the Bennetts.

An old copper penny from Richmond Town was found in the woman's bag.

Santa Anna was a good friend of Gilbert Thompson, son-in-law of Governor Tompkins of New York.

Santa Anna tried to return to Mexico but was not allowed to enter the country.

In 1989, sisters Laurie and Cella find a book of poems with a letter under the cover. It had belonged to the dead woman and was written to her husband.

READ: <u>Mystery of the Strange Traveler</u> by Phyllis Whitney, MacMillan, 1951.

CLUE CARD THREE

The Old Bennett House stands near the restored village of Richmond Town on Staten Island.

Mrs. Bennett gave shelter and care to the ill woman and her child.

Gilbert Thompson gave Santa Anna a home on Staten Island after the General's defeat in Mexico.

Santa Anna wanted to return to Mexico from Staten Island.

Clyde Dibney married a girl from Texas. She was a young widow.

Clyde Dibney was aboard the schooner when it was wrecked.

READ: <u>Mystery of the Strange Traveler</u> by Phyllis Whitney, MacMillan, 1951.

CLUE CARD FOUR

The stagecoach driver was seeking help for a very sick woman and her baby.

The last words spoken by the dying woman were "butcher" and "Alma."

The dead woman's first husband was killed by Santa Anna's troops at the Battle of the Alamo.

Clyde Dibney was disowned by his family as he was frequently mixed up in unsavory episodes.

Laurie and Cella examined the room where the woman had died over 100 years earlier but found no other clues to her identity.

READ: <u>Mystery of the Strange Traveler</u> by Phyllis Whitney, MacMillan, 1951.

THE LITERATURE OF WORLD WAR II

1. Vocabulary Here are words connected with World War II in Europe. Work with a partner. Before each word below write the number of the heading under which you think it belongs. Guess if you do not know. Then read the paragraph that follows to support or deny your guesses. The headings are: **1. people   2. places   3. equipment   4. aircraft**
5. a defense or offense strategy

_____ Convoy	_____ Axis	_____ Blitzkrieg	_____ RAF
_____ Coventry	_____ Dorniers	_____ Allies	_____ Blenheim
_____ Jerry	_____ Luftwaffe	_____ Incendiaries	_____ Blackout
_____ Radar	_____ Lorries	_____ Spitfires	_____ Stukas

The blitzkrieg had ended. The wheels of the lorries carrying the injured no longer turned on the streets of Coventry. The Home Guard welcomed the respite from seeking the injured buried under buildings hit by incendiaries from the Stuka bombers of Hitler's Luftwaffe. But German Dorniers and Stukas were still in the air. The RAF flying Blenheims and Spitfires were ready to fly over Germany and give the Jerries a taste of their own medicine. By 1943 it was England's turn, with the help of American pilots, to bomb Germany.

2. The Pre Reading Journal

Before beginning a novel, students select one pre reading journal sentence starter to write about for five to ten minutes. Writing is shared orally in small groups.

The sentence starters that follow can be used for <u>Blitzcat</u> by Robert Westall (Scholastic, 1989).

A black cat travels through war-torn England in search of her master and touches the lives of those she meets.

<u>The Snow Goose</u> by Paul Gallico (Knopf 1948) A young girl and a hunchback form a friendship which ends when he dies at Dunkirk saving the trapped army there.

Sample open-ended sentence starters.

1. A handicapped person in war time . . .   3. News reports about war can be . . .

2. Wildlife in war torn areas . . .   4. Fear and courage go together when . . .

3. The Literary Book Report

Summarize the novel in six sentences. Include accurate details in a literary description that includes the following:

1. Alliteration: Repeating beginning sounds.

2. Simile: Comparing two things using like or as.

3. Metaphor: Comparing without the use of like or as.

4. Personification: Giving life to nonliving things.

5. Imagery: Using taste, touch, smell, sight and/or hearing to describe.

6. Repetition: Repeating phrases for emphasis.

RESEARCH ORGANIZER

ACTION (Choose one)	Choose a topic Choose a verb Choose a product Make a research statement	PRODUCT (Choose one)

ACTION
(Choose one)

Knowledge
    Define
    Record
    Label
    List

Comprehension
    Summarize
    Describe
    Locate
    Report

Application
    Solve
    Demonstrate
    Dramatize
    Show

Analysis
    Compare
    Categorize
    Classify
    Discover

Synthesis
    Compose
    Hypothesize
    Predict
    Create

Evaluation
    Judge
    Rank order
    Criticize
    Recommend

TOPICS
(Choose One)

I. Causes of Conflict

II. Wartime Leaders
    Stalin, Joseph
    Chamberlain, Neville
    Churchill, Winston
    DeGaule, Charles
    Hitler, Adolph

III. Battles-Strategies
    Dunkerque
    Russian Front
    V-E Day
    Battle of Britain

IV. The Secret War
    Spies
    Underground

V. Conferences and Treaties
    Casablanca
    Potsdam
    Yalta
    Munich Agreement
    Atlantic Charter

VI. Aftermath of War
    Nuremberg Trials
    United Nations

PRODUCT
(Choose one)

Acrostic poem
Advice letter
Autobiography
Bio-poem
Chart
Choral reading
Collage
Comic strip
Concert reading
Diorama
Editorial
Essay
Eyewitness report
Fable
Filmstrip
Interview
Journal
Lesson
Map
Model
Moment in history script
Mystery person report
Newspaper
Oral report
Poem
Question/answer session
Reader's theatre script
Report
Song
Story
Tape recording
Time line
TV script
True/false book

ACTION	TOPIC	PRODUCT
Describe	**the Battle of Britain**	**in an acrostic poem**

AMERICAN HISTORY IN PICTURE BOOKS AND NOVELS

Turn jacket blurbs, which are not copyrighted, into plays to introduce historical eras through picture books and novels.

RESEARCH IDEA Before performing any of the booktalks/plays/scripts in this section, students should research additional information about the time, place or person and share that information at the end of the booktalk

IN THE BEGINNING: NATIVE AMERICAN MYTHS
The First Strawberries: A Cherokee Story retold by Joseph Bruchac. **Illustrated by Anna Vojtech. Dial, 1993.**

N1=Narrator One   N2=Narrator Two   M=Man   W=Woman   S=Sun

N1: How was it that strawberries came into the world? This is how:
N2: Long ago when the world was new the creator made a man and a woman. They
M & W: married and for a long time lived together and were happy.
N2: Yet one day the couple quarreled and the woman
W: left the man in anger and haste.
N1: To stop the woman's flight, the sun
S: sent to Earth raspberries, then blueberries, then blackberries.

Coyote Places the Stars by H. Taylor. Bradbury, 1993.
N1: One evening crafty Coyote
C: climbs to the moon to discover the secrets of the heavens.
N1: Instead he finds a way
C: to make the most wonderful pictures for all the world to see.
N2: When the other animals of the canyon
C: look up at the sky the next night
N2: they are in for a big surprise in this tale of the origin of the constellations.

Activity Create a Coyote **Data Bank**

Eats	Lives	Has	Does
rabbits	in packs	bark or howl	hunts to survive
deer	in the forest	long tail	kills sick animals
fox	in the desert	thick fur	shares work
mice		fear of humans	talks with ears

Activity Complete this **pattern** with information from the data bank.

I am Coyote. See me (3 things) _____ _____ _____

Hear me (3 things) Watch me (3 things) _____

But watch out! I may be watching you!
                              or
Activity Write a **Five Senses Poem** about the desert.

   The desert is _____ (color)   It looks like _____

   It sounds like _____   It tastes like _____

   It smells like _____   It makes me feel like _____

THE EARLY SETTLERS

Samuel Eaton's Day: A Day in the Life of a Pilgrim Boy by Kate Walters. Photo by Russ Kendall. Scholastic Hardcover, 1993.

N1 = Narrator One N2 = Narrator 2 S = Samuel F = Father

N1: Samuel Eaton has
S: hardly slept from excitement.
N1: Today is the day he will help with his
S: first rye harvest.
N1: If he can prove to his father that he's up to the task he will
S: be able to help with all of the harvest. But daily chores must be done before leaving the village with the grown-ups. There's water to fetch, and a snare to check in the woods and kindling to gather for Mam.
N2: When at last it's time to begin
F: harvesting the rye the task proves even more difficult than Samuel expected. His hands
S: are becoming sore and blistered
N1: and the sun has begun to burn his skin. And the straw in his breeches and down his neck makes him
S: itch all over!
N1: Samuel mustn't let Father see how he is struggling.
N2: Was he foolish to think he
S: could do a man's work?
All: Find out when you read Samuel Eaton's Day.

Activity Compare a day in your life with one day in Samuel Eaton's life.

THE AMERICAN REVOLUTION

Katie's Trunk by Ann Turner. Illustrated by Ronald Himler. Macmillan, 1992.

N1=Narrator One N2=Narrator Two M=Mother F=Father R=Rebel

N1: Katie could feel it in the air
F: the way a horse knows a storm is near. Something was wrong.
M: Tories!
N2: Katie's mother said
M: it was because of the tea that was dumped in the harbor, and other things.
N2: Then one day the Rebels came. Katie's father told the family
F: to hide in the woods.
N1: as Katie crouched in the underbrush she
F: got mad and ran back into the house. It's not right to treat good people this way,
N1: she thought as she climbed into a big trunk to hide.
N2: The Rebels came into the house and one
R: reached for the lid of the trunk.
All: To find if Katie is discovered, read Katie's Trunk.

Activity How many different sentences can you write using this **pattern**?

  1. Tea is just tea until it _____ and then it becomes _____.
  2. A ship is just a ship until it _____ and then it becomes _____.
  3. A trunk is just a trunk until it _____ and then it becomes _____.

Johnny Tremain by Esther Forbes. Houghton-Mifflin, 1943.
Reading Parts: N1=Narrator One   N2=Narrator Two   J= Johnny

N1: The year is 1773. The scene is Boston. Johnny Tremain
J: is fourteen and apprenticed to a silversmith.
N1: He is gifted
J: and knows it.
N1: He is lively and clever
J: and holds it over the other apprentices until the tragic day when a crucible of molten
         silver breaks
N2: and Johnny's right hand is so burned as to be useless. Johnny feels that his life is over.
         Then Johnny became
J: a Dispatch Rider and took part in the events that were to lead to the Boston Tea Party
         and the Battle of Lexington.
N2 : There on the battlefield Johnny learns his hand can be healed so that he
J: can use a musket.
N1: To discover what the future holds for Johnny during this most exciting time in
         American history, read Johnny Tremain.

Activity Research the life of Christopher Reeve or another severely handicapped person.
Write a letter from the handicapped person to Johnny. What would he or she tell Johnny?

THE WILDERNESS TRAIL.

A critical listening activity. Readers Theatre. By careful listening students will discover the real Jemima Boone.

Hostess: Loretta Bore
   Welcome everyone to our show. Only one eyewitness is telling the complete truth. It is up to you to guess which it is. Now let's meet our guests.
Eyewitness #1:
   My name is Jemima Boone and I was an eyewitness to the siege of Boonesborough, September 7, 1778.
Eyewitness #2:
   My name is Jemima Boone. I was an eyewitness to the siege of Boonesborough on September 7, 1777, along with my husband, Daniel.
Eyewitness #3:
   My name is Jemima Boone, wife of Daniel Boone and I was an eyewitness to the siege of Boonesborough on September 7, 1778.
Bore: Eyewitness #1, tell us your story.
Eyewitness #1:
   We only had about 50 men and boys to protect us against 400 braves led by Chief Black Fish. It was a fearsome sight . . . then Black Fish asked for a parley. Alone and unarmed, Daniel Boone went out to meet them.
Eyewitness #2:
   Somehow a peace treaty was hammered out, but before it could be signed, the Indians grabbed father. But he threw Black Fish to the ground and was shot in the shoulder getting back to the fort.
Eyewitness #3:
   The Indians cut the telegraph wires. Then they massed for a charge on the North wall. The women and children were hidden away in case the Indians broke through.
Loretta Bore:
   Now it is time to decide who is the real eyewitness to the siege of Boonesborough. We will vote by a show of hands. Is it #1? (Wait for a show of hands) Is it #2? (Wait for a show of hands) Is it #3? (Wait for a show of hands). Now for the moment you have all been waiting for. Will the real Jemima Boone, eyewitness to the siege of Boonesborough, please step forward.

Activity Wilderness Words
Form teams with 2-3 members on a team. One member from each team will choose three words from the Jemima Boone script to act out for his or her team. No words are spoken. A one minute time limit is set for acting out each word. The team that guesses the most words within the time limit is the winner. Suggested words are: siege, wife, treaty, father, Indians, fort, telegraph

THE STAR SPANGLED BANNER

By the Dawn's Early Light by Steven Kroll. Illustrated by Dan Andreasen. Scholastic Hardcover, 1994.

N1=Narrator One   N2=Narrator Two   K=Key

N1: It was only days after the British had burned a defenseless Washington that Francis Scott Key

K: learned that a good friend, Dr. William Beanes, was being held captive on board a British ship.

N1: Driven by devotion to his friend and his country, Key

K: obtained presidential permission to visit the British fleet to request the release of Dr. Beanes.

N2: But to his horror he was forced to stay

K: on board the ship as it attacked Fort McHenry. From the deck of the enemy ship

N2: Key watched helplessly as the British bombed the American fort.

N1: By the dawn's early light Key saw

K: the American flag flying over the fort and was inspired to write the words to the song that would become

All: The National Anthem.

Activity Make a list of patriotic songs. Take a poll of classmates. Which song is the favorite? Titles might include: "This Land Is Your Land," "America the Beautiful," "God Bless America," "The Star Spangled Banner," "Yankee Doodle," "The Battle Hymn of the Republic," "My Country Tis of Thee."

TALL TALE HEROES OF AMERICA'S EARLY DAYS

The Narrow Escapes of Davy Crockett by Ariane Dewey. Greenwillow, 1989.

Activity Using all of the letters in DAVY CROCKETT, create a new adventure for Davy and relate it as an acrostic poem.

D own the Mississippi
A terrible storm made Davy
V ery nervous so he
Y anked a bolt of lightning from the sky, hopped on and rode away.

Mike Fink retold and illustrated by Steven Kellogg. Morrow, 1992.
N1=Narrator One N2=Narrator Two M= Mike

N1: Mike Fink, keelboat man was
M: the most daring and rugged frontiersman on the river.
N1: A runaway at two days old, Mike
M: grew up to be a king of the keelboatmen
N2: the strong, rowdy men who floated cargo down river to New Orleans and poled heavy boats against the current.
N1: But first Mike became a crackerjack marksman with his gun, Bang-All,
M: then grappled with grizzlies.
N2: No man, alligator or snapping turtle could out do the mighty Mike Fink.
N1: That is until
All: Hilton P. Blathersby and his powerful smoke-spewing steamboat came along.
N2: Discover what happens
N1: in this rollicking version of
All: Mike Fink.

Activity Create your own Mike Fink **tall tale**. Follow directions below. First, think of a word for each of the fifteen listed items (Use the name, Mike Fink, for items 5, 7, and 14)
Name: 1. a size 2. a color 3. an animal 4. a place to sleep 5. Mike Fink 6. way to travel
7. Mike Fink 8. something to read 9. same as #3 10. animal noise 11. animal (not #3)
12. animal 13. animal 14. Mike Fink 15. same as #6.

Substitute the words above for the numbers in the story that follows.

  Beside the mighty Mississippi there was a (1) (2) (3) who was sound asleep on a (4). (5) approached on a (6). (7) was reading a (8) and stumbled over the (9) who awakened and gave a loud (10) that frightened the other river animals including the (11), (12) and (13).
(14) left quickly on (15) vowing never to disturb the river animals again.

LET MY PEOPLE GO

Nettie's Trip South **by Ann Turner. MacMillan, 1987.**

13-year-old Nettie travels south with her reporter brother just before the Civil War and observes the injustice of slavery.

Activity Use as many of the items as you can to complete the sentence below:
spinning wheel, rusty spigot, empty bow, tornado, locked safe, door hinge
Injustice is like _____
because _____ .

Escape from Slavery **by Doreen Rappaport. HarperCollins.1991.**

N1 =   Narrator One N2=Narrator Two E=Eliza M=Master

M: "Eliza is to be sold but we'll keep the child."
N1:   The Master's words stunned Eliza. So late that night she
E: wrapped the baby in a blanket and walked all night
N2:   to the frozen river, pathway to freedom.
N1:   But with the daylight
E: the ice had broken up.
N1:   Where would she hide until night? The baby cried out.
M: What was that?
N2:   Eliza heard the Master's voice in the distance. Then she
E: spotted a small cabin.
N1:   Would she find help?
N2:   Or would she be turned over to the Master?
N1:   She must have shelter
E: or the baby would freeze. Fearfully
N1 & N2:she reached up
E: and knocked on the door.

Activity The Two Word Story. Using a team of four, retell Eliza's story with each team member using only two words at a time.

MOVING WEST

Wagon Wheels by Barbara Brenner. Illustrated by Don Bolognese. HarperCollins, 1993.

N1=Narrator One, N2=Narrator Two, F=Family, E=Ed

N1: Wagon Wheels is based on a true story. In 1878, Ed Muldie
E: left Kentucky to go to Kansas
N2: with his family. They
E: had heard about the Homestead Act, which promised free land to anyone willing to settle the West.
N1: Many black pioneers like the Muldies
F: settled in Kansas.
N2: The boys in this story
F: stayed alone in a dugout and traveled 150 miles
N2: by themselves to find their father.
N1: The family faced
F: starvation, freezing cold, rattlesnakes, wild animals, and prairie fires but survived it all
All: to make a home on the prairie.

Activity Rank the Danger! **Rank order** these dangers faced by prairie families from most dangerous to least dangerous. Defend your ranking.
___ prairie fires
___ wild animals (wolves, panthers, coyotes)
___ prairie rattlesnakes
___ freezing snows
___ starvation

Activity Improv! Classmates write 4-5 word phrases on small slips of paper. The phrases should have something to do with traveling West in the 1800s. Two students taking the role of travelers begin a conversation. Each must pick up (in turn) and use in his or her conversation three of the phrases.

THE TRAIL OF TEARS

Sing Down the Moon by Scott O'Dell. Houghton-Mifflin, 1970.

Reading Parts: N1=Narrator One N2=Narrator Two S=Soldiers B= Bright Morning
T=Tall Boy

N1: The spring that came to the Canyon de Chelly in 1864 was abundant, for the fields and orchards of the Navahos who lived there promised a rich harvest.
N2: The sheep were lambing and the sky was bright blue.
N1: But all was shattered when the white soldiers
S: burned the crops, destroyed the fruit trees, and forced the Navahos out of the canyon
B/T: to join others on the devastating long march to Fort Sumner.
N1: Through the eyes of Bright Morning, a young Navaho girl, we see
B: what can happen to human beings when they are uprooted from the life they know.
N1: She tells the story
B: of the proud and able Tall Boy,
N2: the youth she expected to marry, who is
T: maimed not only by a physical wound, but a spiritual wound as well.
N1: And she tells of the other men of the tribe
B: who on the march along the "Trail of Tears" lose their will along with their way of life.
N2: It is a story with tragic overtones,
B: a story of the breaking of the human spirit.
N1: And yet, fortunately, then as now, there were a few possessed of inner strength based on hope; Bright Morning was one of these.

Activity Both Bright Morning and Tall Boy changed from the beginning to the end of the novel. The **free verse** that follows describes the changes in Tall Boy. Use the same pattern to describe the changes in Bright Morning.

Example

Tall Boy

You are changing, changing
You feel the shackles of defeat like
a vice around your neck
You are angry and grief-stricken
You clench your fist and shout to the sky
You are diminished in your tallness as the guns of
the white soldiers are trained upon your people
You do not walk upright anymore
As you hear women wailing, children crying and
proud men bending under the Army's yoke.
It is demeaning to walk like this
As defeated as the wild buffalo
You are an Indian brave on the Trail of Tears

You are changing, changing
You feel: describe the atmosphere
You are: two adjectives
You: two verbs or verb phrases
You: describe how change appears
You do not: what is different?
As you: three participle phrases
It is: adjective and simile
You are: Name

TO A NEW WORLD

Read Wildflower Girl by Marita Conlon-McKenna. Holiday House, 1992.

Reading Parts: Narrator One, Peggy, Mrs. Cavendish, Narrator Two

Narrator One:	Thirteen-year-old Peggy O'Driscoll can find no work in her small village in Ireland so she
Peggy:	sets off on a terrifying voyage to America and arrives in the big city of Boston
Narrator Two:	to find work as a maid to Mrs. Cavendish,
Mrs. Cavendish:	a drunken landlady who runs a boarding house.
Narrator One:	Peggy is
Peggy:	overworked and underfed.
Narrator Two:	Then one night Mrs. Cavendish is missing and the men want their supper.
Narrator One:	Peggy finds
Peggy:	only eggs to cook and fixes them for the men.
Narrator One:	Much later that night Peggy
Peggy:	is awakened by blows from the landlady. She refuses
Mrs. Cavendish:	to listen to Peggy's explanation for the missing eggs and beats the girl severely.
Peggy:	Left alone with a bloody face and a missing tooth
Narrator One:	Peggy vows
Peggy:	to run away.
Narrator Two:	But where will she run to? Signs in every store window say "No Irish Need Apply."
Peggy:	Anything would be better than this,
Narrator One:	Peggy thinks, as she carefully makes her way
Peggy:	down the stairs and out the door.
Narrator Two:	To discover what happens to Peggy and how she makes her place in the New World, read:
ALL:	Wildflower Girl.

Activity How many of these words can you use in **ONE sentence to describe** how Peggy felt and what she saw when she got off the ship in Boston? Add other words as needed.

devastated	misfortune	distinguished	hostile	constable
congenial	blighted	consultation	proclaim	prosperous
remorse	Hibernian	insurrection	trepidation	composure
pandemonium	interrogation	famine	cowering	mockery
agitated	indignation	scrutinize	scoundrel	

Activity Create a book titled H Is for Immigrant. Brainstorm words that are related to immigration that begin with the letter **H**. Each page in the book will explain how each word is connected.

See also: If Your Name Was Changed at Ellis Island by Ellen Levine. Scholastic, 1992 and An Ellis Island Christmas by Maxinne Leighton. Viking, 1992.

AMERICA THE BEAUTIFUL

Neil Waldman has beautifully illustrated the words of Katherine Lee Bates' song, "America the Beautiful." (Atheneum, 1992)

"Oh beautiful, for spacious skies for amber waves of grain,
For purple mountains majesties above the fruited plain
America, America, God shed his grace on thee.
And crown thy good with brotherhood
From sea to shining sea."

Activity Follow the pattern to **write a second verse** about America. Sing to the tune if "Skip to My Lou." **Example**

We see:
Strong people hurrying to work Mighty rivers winding in and out
Many roads stretching across the land Land of the brave and free.

We see

_____ _____ _____ _____
_____ _____ _____ _____
_____ _____ _____ _____

  Land of the brave and free.

Activity Complete this **chant** with adjectives about America.

Sights to see in America

_____rivers

_____plains

_____mountains

_____coasts

_____deserts

_____ ____lakes

These are just a few

_____states

_____land

_____people

_____freedoms

_____cities

_____farms

Minireaps (Mini Research Projects)

Rather than assigning monthly research papers of ten or more pages (which often results in copying and "data dumping") assign a one-half page paper two times a week. Students give their half page report to assigned groups and receive input and questions from the group. Every third week the student hands in the paper he or she feels is his/her best work.

Types of Mini Research Papers

1. **Data Interpretation**
The student will write one-half page telling what a chart, graph or list of data means. Some assumptions may have to be backed up by additional research.

2. **Challenge Literal Fact**
The student researches and writes one-half page to challenge a literal fact.
Example Write one-half page telling why George Washington was the first president of the U.S.

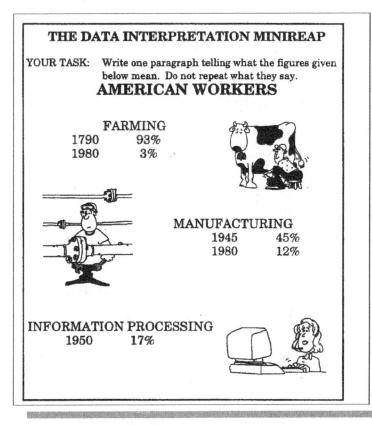

THE DATA INTERPRETATION MINIREAP

YOUR TASK: Write one paragraph telling what the figures given below mean. Do not repeat what they say.

AMERICAN WORKERS

FARMING
1790   93%
1980   3%

MANUFACTURING
1945   45%
1980   12%

INFORMATION PROCESSING
1950   17%

MINIREAP EVALUATION FORM

Circle the number on the line that best shows the success of the writer in dealing with the question.

1. Is the minireap's statement of purpose clear?
NO 1_____2_____3_____4_____5 YES

2. Is the thinking fully developed? (Is equal treatment given to several main ideas?)
NO 1_____2_____3_____4_____5 YES

3. Do the paper's conclusions make sense? Are they logical?
NO 1_____2_____3_____4_____5 YES

4. Are the main points easy to determine?
NO 1_____2_____3_____4_____5 YES

5. Does the minireap show solid evidence (rather than opinion) to support main ideas?
NO 1_____2_____3_____4_____5 YES

6. Do poor grammar or spelling errors interfere with the reader getting the full meaning?
NO 1_____2_____3_____4_____5 YES

NON FICTION AND RESEARCH REPORTING PATTERNS

By about grade four, students in schools with library/media programs have, for the most part, achieved familiarity with the contents of their particular media center and have acquired most of the basic skills of location of library/media materials. It would follow then that by the end of grade four that independent study projects should be a basic part of the curriculum. However, regardless of the skills the student may possess, many research assignments do not call for the utilization of these skills. Teachers bemoan the fact that most students tend to copy information from the encyclopedia or the Internet and that the majority of research assignments are not eagerly approached by students.

The key to moving students from lower to higher levels of thinking in the research activity is product. If we change the product we change the process the student uses to obtain the product. For example, if the student is asked to do a report about a particular state, the typical response is to copy several paragraphs about that state from the encyclopedia. The thinking level used is knowledge. When we change the product we also change the thinking level required. The assignment might be as follows: The White House has called and your family has been selected as the typical family for your state. The President is coming to dinner. Plan a menu. You may serve only those things raised or grown in your state. You may use only ingredients raised or grown in your state.

With the foregoing assignment the student must first locate the information. Second, he or she must analyze the information in order to combine separate elements in a new way (synthesis) to create a menu. Thus the higher levels of thinking are achieved through the changing of the research product.

In the pages that follow students are introduced to many reporting patterns. When students are ready to move from patterns to the clearly written, well-developed report, the "tricks of the non fiction writer's trade" are presented and can be incorporated in report writing on any topic.

HOW TO WRITE EXCITING NON FICTION

Examine various non fiction texts. Look for the following features. Use these same "tricks of the trade" in your own report writing.

1. The author gets your attention by **asking a question or using the word "you"** in the opening sentence.
Wetlands by Marcia Freeman. Newbridge, 1998.
"If **you** visit a wetland wear your boots."
If You Hopped Like a Frog by David Schwartz. Scholastic, 2000.
"If **you** hopped like a frog, **how far could you hop?**"

2. The author tells **what is happening, not what is.**
"Buckingham Fountain shoots a spout of water 150 feet into the skies above Chicago. It gushes from Grant Park, the city's front yard . . . What a front door! What a front yard!"
From Chicago by R. Conrad Stein. Children's Press, 1997.
"I have five sharpened claws on my huge, furry paws. I can walk, I can swim, I can run. If I chase you, watch out! If I see you, take care! I'm grumpy, I'm gruff. I like playing rough. I'm a dangerously dangerous bear." From: Polar Bears by John Parsons. Wright Group, 2001.
"A young river is full of energy. It plunges and falls this way and that down the best path."
From Rivers by David L. Harrison. Boyds Mill, 2002.

3. The author **connects the unfamiliar with something the reader knows.**
"The Great Barrier Reef is like a huge fish tank."
Australia. Carolrhoda Books, 2000.

4. The author tells **who, what, when and where.**
From Gorillas by Josie Stewart and Lynn Salem. Illustrated by Kristi Gerner. Seedling Publications, 2000. Reading Level Two
"You can learn about gorillas in the zoo or in the mountains of Africa. Let's take a look. When the baby gorilla wakes up, she is hungry. She begins to eat the plants around her."

5. The author **gives proof.**
Read the first sentence (or statement) of a non fiction piece. Read the rest of the paragraph. Ask students to identify the details (or proof) for the first statement.
"Trains made the world a different place. Before the invention of the train, long journeys took many weeks or months on foot or wagon."
From Seymour Simon's Book of Trains. HarperCollins, 2002.

6. The author relates events in **sequential order**.

Time Sequence

Samuel Eaton's Day by Kate Waters. Scholastic, 1993.

Follow Samuel of Plimoth Plantation through one day from the time he awakes, fetches water, checks snares in the woods, gathers kindling and at last, leaves with the men for the harvesting of the rye. At the end of the day Samuel returns home, tired with blistered hands, but proud that he has done a man's work.

White Bear, Ice Bear by Joanne Ryder. Morrow, 1989.

A child is magically transformed into an ice bear and lives the life of the bear for one day before returning home at night.

ABC Sequence Learning about birds from A to Z.

The Bird Alphabet Book by Jerry Pallotta. Charlesbridge, 1995.

"A is for Atlantic Puffin. Atlantic Puffins have colorful beaks. They live on the ocean almost all year. When nesting on land they are found in groups called colonies."

Number Sequence

Peas and Potatoes by Michael K. Smith. from the Pair-It Books series published by Steck-Vaughn, 1997.

While the farmer is busy planting and weeding above ground, a hungry mole eats one cabbage, two onions, three potatoes, four pea pods, five beans, and six carrots, and then goes to sleep.

How-To Sequence

A Smiling Salad by Michael K. Smith. from the Pair-It Books series published by Steck-Vaughn, 1997.

A young boy shows step-by-step how to put together a salad resulting in lettuce hair with a smiling face. The face has a carrot nose, tomato eyes and a celery mouth and yellow pepper ears.

Order Sequence

Our Government by Wanda Haan. Rand McNally, 2000.

Beginning with communities the author shows city government, moves to state and then national government in an easy-to-read format.

7. The author uses **alliteration and onomatopoeia**.

When words together have the same beginning sound this is called **alliteration**.

When words create a sound, this is called **onomatopoeia**.

Put an **A** in front of the descriptions that follow if you find alliteration. Put an **O** if you find onomatopoeia. (Can be done orally.)

_____ "The snow gets deeper and deeper. Lawns are white. Trees are white, and so are the roofs of houses. Everything is covered, Everything is white."
From: <u>Snow is Falling</u> by Franklyn Branley. HarperCollins, 1986.

_____ "If you should be in the wild bush lands of the country of Kenya, on the continent of Africa, and you should hear a call – "Weet-err, weet-err" be joyous. Shout "Kumbe!" to the heavens. For you have the good fortune to meet a honey guide,"
From: <u>If Yo u Should Hear a Honey Guide</u> by April Pulley Sayre. Houghton-Mifflin, 1995.

_____ "Right in the middle of busy New York City is a wide wonderful park."
From: <u>Exploring Parks</u> with Ranger Dockett by Alice Flanagan. Children's Press, 1997.

_____ "A frog makes noises so other frogs can hear it. Ribbit, ribbit."
From: <u>From Tadpole to Frog</u> by Jan Kottke. Children's Press, 2000.

_____ "Deep down beneath the world of sunshine, is the dark world of caves."
From: <u>Caves</u> by Larry Dane Brimner. Children's Press, 2000.

_____ "A-GOO-WAH!" High up in the tree tops the howler monkey cries to mark off its territory. You can hear the chilling sound from as far away as two miles."
From: <u>Life in the Rain Forest</u> by Melvin Berger.
Newbridge Educational Publishing, New York, 1993.

EVALUATING NON FICTION

Does the non fiction book:

_____ 1. Begin with a sentence that involves the reader?

_____ 2. Use action words to tell about the subject?

_____ 3. Compare the unknown with something the reader knows?

_____ 4. Present information in an orderly sequence?

_____ 5. Give proof for statements made?

_____ 6. Involve two or more of the five senses?

_____ 7. Tell who, what, when, where?

_____ 8. Include similes? _____ repetition? _____ alliteration? _____ onomatopoeia?

_____ 9. Does the ending use a universal word (everyone, every time, all, etc.)
_____ conclude a sequence or _____ give the reader something to wonder about?

Does the biography:

_____ 1. Have a beginning that "hooks" the reader?

_____ 2. Tell who, what, when and where?

_____ 3. Reveal the person's life with action? (Tells what he or she does.)

_____ 4. Tell what others say about the person?

_____ 5. Tell of the difficulties that were overcome?

_____ 6. Tell of the person's accomplishments?

_____ 7. Use the tools of the writer's craft: _____ alliteration _____ repetition
_____ similes

INFORMATIVE WRITING: PRIMARY GRADES

Knowledge
1. Name the object.   This is a snowflake.

Comprehension
2. Tell where found.   It is found falling from the sky.

Application
3. How can you use it?   People can ski on snow.

Analysis
4. Compare with something else.   Snow falls as flakes but sleet falls as tiny beads.

Synthesis
5. What can you create?   With snowflakes and sugar I can make snow ice cream.

Evaluation
6. Judge   I would rather play in snow than rain because my sled will not go on rain.

Activity Choose one: APPLE, MILK, TREE, BASEBALL CAP

1. Name: _____

2. Where found? It is found_____

3. Uses: _____

4. Compare:_____

5. Create:_____

6. Judge:_____

CATEGORIZING WITH WORD BANKS FOR SONGS AND CHANTS

Brainstorm all the nouns and describing words you can about winter, spring, summer or fall. Use the words in a chant.

WINTER THINGS
Cold winds
Warm fires
Icicles
Fur coats
Warm mittens
Ear muffs
These are just a few
Snow boots
Sleeping bears
Bare trees
White snow
Road cleaners
Dark mornings
Fast sleds, too
From near and far
Here they are
WINTER THINGS!

Use the same pattern to build word banks about any topic
.
EXAMPLE

A Pumpkin Chant

We like pumpkins
Plump pumpkins
Round pumpkins
Yellow pumpkins
Orange pumpkins
Grinning pumpkins
Scary pumpkins
These are just a few
Pumpkin seeds
Pumpkin vines
Pumpkin patches
Pumpkin pie
Pumpkin bread
Pumpkin cake
Jack-o-lanterns, too
Shout hooray
Every day
We like pumpkins

SPRING THINGS

_____
_____
_____
_____
_____
_____

These are just a few

_____
_____
_____
_____
_____
_____, too
From near and far
Here they are
SPRING THINGS!

A _____ Chant
We like_____
_____
_____
_____
_____
_____

These are just a few

_____
_____
_____
_____
_____
_____, too
Shout hooray every day,
We like _____

CHANTS AND SONGS

1. Are You Sleeping

(who?)   Furry Wombat
(who?)   Furry Wombat
(where?) In your burrow
(where?) In Australia
(what?)   Digging and eating
(what?)   Watching and climbing
(when?)   Only at night
(when?)   Only at night.

2. Skip to My Lou

A wombat has a pouch and hide
A wombat has long fur and claws
A wombat has small ears and whiskers
And comes out at night.

3. London Bridge

Nightingales eat bugs and spiders,
Bugs and spiders,
Bugs and spiders,
Nightingales eat bugs and spiders
And sing beautiful songs.

4. I'm a Little Teapot

(transformation report)
Look at the flower that grows from a seed
Slowly. slowly from a seed
In the garden it grew and grew
Look at the flower its brand new.

REPORTING PATTERNS

1. Another transformation pattern
An Egg is an Egg by Nicki Weiss. Putnam's, 1990.

An egg is an egg until it hatches and then it becomes a chick.

A _____ is a _____ until it _____

and then it becomes a _____ .

2. Reporting on ocean creatures
   I saw a_____ and the _____ saw me,

   It was _____ along in the deep blue sea

_____ goes_____, _____, _____ .
   I saw a whale and the whale saw me
   It was swimming along in the deep blue sea.
   Whale goes whoosh, whoosh, whee!

3. The simile report
The Sleepy Book by Charlotte Zolotow. HarperCollins, 1989.
   The snowy crane sleeps standing on one long leg like a flower on its stem.
   (factual statement plus simile)

4. Five Senses Report
   Color: The Emerald City is green
   Sound: It sounds like a beautiful orchestra
   Taste: It tastes like mint candy
   Smell: It smells like poppy flowers
   Sight: It looks like a sparkling jewel box
   Feeling: It makes me feel like singing.

5. Reporting on a country, state or province

If I visited the country of _____

I could _____

And I'd _____

And _____

But I couldn't _____ because visitors to _____ do that.

If I visited the State of Missouri
I could see the Gateway Arch
And I'd ride on a Clydesdale horse at Grant's Farm
And swim in the Lake of the Ozarks
But I wouldn't visit Lincoln's tomb
Because visitors to Illinois do that.

6. Use the pattern from A My Name is Alice by Jane Bayer. Dutton, 1984.
A my name is Andrea
My husband's name is Alex
We come from Arizona
And we sell avocados. apricots and art
Andrea is an armadillo
Alex is an angleworm.
(Products and animals must be native to the place.)

7. Coming Round the Mountain
(Choose a state or country to research)
She'll be coming from (Capital) when she comes
She'll be coming from (large city) when she comes
She'll be bringing (three products)
She'll be bringing (three crops)
She'll be coming from (State or Country) when she comes.

8. Biography Report

If I were Michael Jordan
I would be a famous basketball player
And I would help win many games
But I wouldn't win golf tournaments
Because Tiger Woods **does that**.

9. Animal Report

Choose an animal_____

Tell two things it has._____   _____

Tell two things it does._____   _____

Tell where you would find the animal_____
Use the information in a song.
Tune: "A Hunting We Will Go"

Example

A lion has a mane
A lion has four legs
A lion roars, a lion hunts
And lives in Africa.

10. Reporting on a Place

Choose a city, state or country to read about. List four sights you would see if you went walking in that place. Use the four sights in this song: Tune: "This Land Is Your Land."

As I went walking in _____

I saw _____ and _____

I saw the _____ and the _____

Sights that everyone should see.

180

11. The Important Pattern

Begin with the statement: "The important thing about _____ is . . .
Follow this statement with three to six details about the topic. Then repeat the first line.

Example

The important thing about the work of Thomas Edison **is** that he invented the electric light. He only went through the third grade. His teachers thought he was learning disabled. He worked as a telegraph operator and accidentally started a fire on a train.
But the important thing about Thomas Edison **is** that he invented the electric light.

12. List Report

We like eggs!
  Robin's eggs
  Snake eggs
  Crocodile eggs
  Ostrich eggs
  Turtle eggs
  Penguin eggs
These are just a few.
  In a nest
  In a hole
  In the swamp
  Along the dunes
  In the sand
  In the snow
Scrambled eggs, too!
  Stand and shout.
  Bring them out.
  We like eggs!

13. Process Pattern

COTTON

I WONDER WHY THEY . . .
  Prepare the soil
  Plant the seeds
  Cultivate the earth
  Spray the crops
  Pick the cotton
  Remove the fibers
  Bale the lint
  Truck the bales
  Clean the cotton
  Spin the thread
  Weave the yarn
  Dye the cloth
  Cut and sew
When I could wear
WOOL INSTEAD!

Wombat Chant

Facts about wombats
Has a pouch
Tough hide
Long fur
Sharp claws
Small ears
Whiskers
These are just a few.
Vegetable eater
Carries young
Good pet
Digs burrows
Yellow-black
Night creature
Eats leaves, too.
From near and far,
Here they are,
Facts about wombats!

A Taco Speaks
I have never
understood
why anyone would
roast the shell
buy the meat
chip the pickles
chop the lettuce
when they could
sit back
and call . . .
Chicken Delight! ! !

14.   A Listing Response
I see snakes:
        spotted snakes, striped snakes, black
        snakes, green snakes
I see snakes in places
        under rocks, in the grass, on the water,
        up a tree
I see doing snakes
        wriggling snakes, crawling snakes,
        slithering snakes, sunning snakes
I see snakes.

15. An Attribute Report

I am rattlesnake, hear me
 Swish through the sand
 Lift my tail
 Shake my rattles
I am rattlesnake, see my
 Yellow cover, diamond blotches, seven foot length, horny rattles
I am rattlesnake, watch me
 Sun myself, uncoil my body, shake my rattles, strike a rodent with my sharp fangs
I am rattlesnake, hear me, see me, watch me, but watch out! I may be watching you!

16. Compare/Contrast Pattern

If I had the _____ of a _____
I would _____
And I'd _____
But I wouldn't _____
And _____
Because _____ (do/does) that.

Example

If I had the faithfulness of Horton
I would sit on an egg for a year
And I'd always keep my promises
no matter how difficult the task.
But I wouldn't fly away and take a vacation when there's work to be done
For Mayzie the lazy bird does that.

17. Action Pattern

If I were in charge of _____
There would be _____
You wouldn't have _____
I'd cancel _____
But the most important thing I would do is _____
_____

18. Descriptive Pattern

Hey kids! I have a _____ for sale.
It's the handiest thing you will ever
want to own since it can _____
and _____
and _____
and the greatest thing about it is_____
_____

19. "If I Were" Pattern"

Name the thing you want to be. _____

Where is it found? _____

One thing it would do for someone else. _____

A second thing it would do. _____

  Repeat the first line.

Example

  If I were a blanket
  All snug in your bed
  I would curl all around you
  And keep you warm from toe to head
  If I were a blanket.

20. Fortunately/Unfortunately

Fortunately George Washington Carver revolutionized the agriculture of the South.

Unfortunately he was born of slave parents and lost his mother to a band of night raiders.

Fortunately he was able to attend Simpson College.

Unfortunately he had to earn his way by cooking, taking in laundry and working as a janitor,

Fortunately he received an appointment at Iowa State University as an assistant botanist.

Unfortunately he made very little money during his lifetime.

Fortunately he discovered over 300 uses for the peanut and received the Roosevelt Medal for his many contributions to science.

21. The Acrostic

  War correspondent
  In South Africa, 1899
  Notorious Boer enemy
  Seizes armored
  Train
  Of those aboard, he is captured.
  No hope of escape.

  Checks out prison camp.
  High walls, floodlights, sentries.
  Up, over the wall, in an unguarded moment
  Racing heart, he scales the heights,
  Camp left behind.
  Hopping railroad cars
  In dead of night finds British help.
  Lauded as a hero.
  Leader of the future.

22. The Who, What, When, Where, Why Acrostic

(who)	**S**nakes come in many colors
(what)	**N**on poisonous and poisonous
(when)	**A**lthough many hibernate in winter
(where)	**K**eeping out of sight underground
(why)	**E**very night gaining energy.

23. The Metaphor/Simile Acrostic

Slithers smoothly as the slippery eel
Necktie of brilliant colors
As silent as the rising sun
Kaleidoscope of changing patterns
Exile from human society.

24. Limerick

Jesse James

A bandit he was sure enough
So daring so bold and so tough
He said,"Give me your money,
I'm not being funny,
My boys and I always play rough."

25. Bio Poem

Line		
1	First name	Gretel
2	Four traits	Small, lost, tired, hungry
3	Related to	Sister of Hansel
4	Cares deeply about	Cares deeply about her family
5	Who feels	Who feels afraid
6	Who needs	Who needs a place to sleep
7	Who gives	Who gives companionship
8	Who fears	Who fears the witch
9	Who would like to see	Who would like to see father again
10	Resident of	Resident of the forest

(Hansel and Gretel)

26. Describing Places: Preposition Poem

IN the tropical rain forest
OVER ropy vines that frame the views and rain that pokes
through narrow slots
ABOVE the rotting limbs and logs filled with the chirps of frogs
BETWEEN giant forest trees
Stalks the graceful jaguar.

27. Resume Pattern

NAME: African Lion

HEIGHT: five to eight feet

WEIGHT: 350-550 pounds

DIET: Giraffes, warthogs and an occasional baby elephant for dessert

HOBBIES: Practicing great leaps and loud roars

DISPOSITION: Generally peaceful unless hungry or challenged

ACCOMPLISHMENTS: Star of the MGM logo for motion pictures

28. Recipe

1 cup talented athlete

2 tablespoons physics and English degrees

½ cup astrophysics Ph.D.

1 slice astronaut application

2 large packages NASA

Mix spacecraft with

1 female flight engineer

Cook for six days, testing robot arms frequently

Remove Challenger from atmosphere

Preserve Sally Ride as the first American woman in space

29. Ten Reasons Report

Ten Reasons to be a Volcano

1. You never have to wait your turn to erupt.
2. Free centralized heating
3. People hundreds of miles away pay attention to you.
4. You don't have to fly to Hawaii.
5. You don't need growth hormones.
6. Your ash makes rich soil for growing things.
7. You can claim ownership of 80% of the Earth's surface.
8. You can sleep as late as you want. No one will wake you up.
9. For your birthday you have 499 relatives to remember you.
10. You'll have a blast!

30. Geography Riddle Report

(Use to describe a place or an historical event)

Let's go to far away places

And see history's changing faces.

(List six to eight items)

A crowded beach with the muck and stink of smoke overhead

With Jerry bullets and bombs behind and above

And off shore the Kentish maid

But no was to get to the boat.

Then a destroyer comes up with ack ack and pom poms.

And between the bullets they come, small boats of every description.

But that's not all

(6-8 more items)

From 100 miles across the North Sea

They sailed through frothin' water and shell splashes to save us

The wounded went first

Some died so that others could escape

Beaten but unconquered they faced the enemy

And democracy shone in all its splendor.

Where am I? (Dunkirk, 1940)

31. Reporting with Free Verse

You are changing, changing.

You feel:	describe the atmosphere
You are:	two adjectives
You:	two verbs or verb phrases
You are:	color
the color of:	name an object the same color
You are:	give size and shape
and are:	use participle and prepositional phrase

You do not walk upright anymore

as you:	three verb phrases
It is:	adjective (to move like this)
so:	one adjective and one simile
You are:	name.

You are changing, changing. **You feel** a harsh cold wind whip across your face, but you don't mind because **you are** strong and furry. **You** sing to the moon and roam through the Arctic wilderness without fear and without a map. **You are** gray, **the color of** fog. **You are** six feet long from nose to tail tip **and are** trotting across the Polar Ice Pack toward a distant herd of caribou on shore, your claws clicking with each step you take. **You do not walk upright anymore as you** hunt for snow-white rabbits, lope silently past Polar bears sniffing the air, and crawl into your home beneath an outcropping of rocks. **It is** wild to move like this so free and **so** secret like a dream. **You are** an Arctic wolf.

32. Mystery Report

(Use for person, place or thing)

List ten things about the topic. Mix up the clues. One must be a give away clue. Ask a volunteer to give a number between 1 and 10. Read the clue for that number. The person can guess or pass. Ask for more volunteers until all clues are read or the topic is guessed.

33. Use this model to report about a person or event

THE TV SHOW: TO TEST THE TRUTH

(The audience decides on the real eyewitness)

HOSTESS: Welcome, everyone to our show. Only one eyewitness is telling the complete truth. It is up to you to decide who it is. Now let's meet our guests.

EYEWITNESS #1: My name is Molly Brown and I was an eyewitness to the sinking of the Titanic. I was reading in my stateroom when I felt a great jolt. We had hit an iceberg.

EYEWITNESS #2: My name is Molly Brown. I was traveling with my husband, James, when there was this terrible crash. We were all ordered to the lifeboats. James pushed people aside so I could get to a boat.

EYEWITNESS #3: My name is Mrs. James J. Brown and I was a passenger on the Titanic when it hit something and began to sink. I made it to a lifeboat manned by a drunken sailor.

HOSTESS: What else can you tell us?

EYEWITNESS #1: There was such panic, and since I had never learned to read I could not read the instructions given us as to what to do in an emergency. I felt so helpless!

EYEWITNESS #2: I had no one to depend on but myself so I grabbed my mink coat and made it to a lifeboat before the Titanic went under.

EYEWITNESS #3: The sailor in our boat did nothing to help the frightened people so I took charge. I got them to singing and rowing to keep their spirits up.

HOSTESS: Now it is time to vote by a show of hands. Is it #1? #2? #3? Now for the moment you have all been waiting for. Will the real Molly Brown, eyewitness to the sinking of the Titanic, please stand up.